Compendium 2012

Compendium 2012

Art Department Faculty Exhibition

Chazen Museum of Art, 2012

University of Wisconsin–Madison

ISBN 13: 978-1-933270-15-9
ISBN 10: 1-933270-15-2

Library of Congress Cataloging-in-Publication Data

Compendium 2012 : Art Department Faculty Exhibition.
    pages cm
  This book is published on the occasion of Compendium 2012: Art Department Faculty Exhibition at the Chazen Museum of Art, University of Wisconsin-Madison, February 4-April 1, 2012. T
  ISBN 978-1-933270-15-9 (alk. paper)
  1. Art, American—Wisconsin—Madison—21st century—Exhibitions. 2. University of Wisconsin—Madison. Dept. of Art—Faculty—Exhibitions. I. Chazen Museum of Art.

  N6535.M33C66 2012
  709.775'8307477583—dc23

                                    2011052565

Cover: UW Art Lofts. Photo: Jim Escalante
Catalogue edited by Susan Day
Designed by Jeff Weyer

contents

Foreword

Since 1974, the Chazen Museum of Art (then the Elvehjem Museum of Art) has presented periodic exhibitions of the work of University of Wisconsin–Madison art faculty. Generally held every four years, these comprehensive exhibitions showcase the achievements of individual faculty members and highlight artistic developments in the department as a whole. Each exhibition is new and exciting. Many longer-term faculty members have explored new art forms since the last exhibition, and the work of new faculty members is introduced to our community. One constant is the broad range of media—painting, drawing, sculpture, graphic arts, ceramics, woodworking, metalworking, glassmaking, textiles, printmaking, photography, installation, video, and computer-generated art—that is practiced and taught on campus. The exhibition not only reflects the creativity and dynamism of the Art Department itself but also the current national art scene.

This year's exhibition, *Compendium 2012: Art Department Faculty Exhibition*, is being presented throughout the museum—in the temporary exhibition galleries of both the new building that opened in October 2011 and in the Conrad A. Elvehjem building. It showcases recent work by the 34 current faculty, staff, and affiliates, as well as 12 emeriti faculty. Each artist selected his or her own work to be exhibited; given the nature of each individual's work, the actual number of works displayed varies from individual to individual. Michael Connors, Tom Loeser, Paul Sacaridiz, and Elaine Scheer comprised the exhibition's steering committee, which worked closely with the museum's exhibition coordinator Mary Ann Fitzgerald to establish the basic parameters of the exhibition and facilitate its implementation.

The present catalogue was beautifully designed by Jeff Weyer, and adeptly edited by the Chazen's editor, Susan Day. Jerl Richmond, the museum's exhibition designer, also deserves special acknowledgment. It is no easy task to coordinate and elegantly place works of various media, sizes, and artistic orientation, by so many different artists, in a single exhibition.

Others whose efforts were particularly instrumental to the successful outcome of this complex project are: Ann Sinfield and Andrea Selbig, the museum's registrars; Anne Lambert, the curator for education; and Steve Johanowicz and Kate Wanberg, installation specialists. In addition, of course, all the museum staff, as members of our highly effective team, were contributors. Where would we be without the events organizers, accountants, and administrative support?

Funding for this exhibition was generously provided by the Chazen Museum of Art Council, the Brittingham Fund, the UW–Madison School of Education, and the Wisconsin Arts Board with funds from the State of Wisconsin and the National Endowment for the Arts.

Russell Panczenko
Director, Chazen Museum of Art

Foreword

It is a great pleasure to welcome you to *Compendium 2012: Art Department Faculty Exhibition*. Since 1974 the Art Department faculty have periodically shared our work with the university and Madison communities.

Since our last exhibit in 2008, five new faculty members have joined our department. In 2009 Fred Stonehouse joined the drawing/painting area. This past fall, four new assistant professors started together: Leslie Smith III in drawing and painting; Meg Mitchell, in digital foundations and advanced digital and electronic media; Matthew Bakkom, in photography; and Sarah FitzSimons, in sculpture. These five have contributed a wonderful new energy to the department. You can see the work of the four newest professors featured on the exhibition announcement.

We miss two of our esteemed colleagues who have retired from teaching: Truman Lowe and Carol Pylant. Since our last exhibition we have lost emeritus professors Robert Grilley, Skip Johnson, Ron Neperud, and Richard Reese. Everyone in the department was also deeply saddened by the loss of Professor Gelsey Verna in 2008.

Our amazing office staff continues to evolve. Melissa Cooke, our front desk manager and perpetrator of brilliant "Dress Up Wednesday" events, has moved on to develop her already successful artistic career. We wish her luck, although we also know she will make her own. Jennifer Simonelli has joined us in the office, taking on many tasks including an expansion of our outreach to alumni and to the campus community and beyond.

In 2009 we moved many Art Department facilities into the new Art Lofts, near the Kohl Center. The Lofts houses graduate-student and faculty studios, a glass lab, metal sculpture foundry, ceramics, papermaking, and digital photography facilities, as well as a great new gallery and open, bright public spaces. We are very pleased with the usability of the building and the way the layout encourages social interaction and discourse. We look forward to having Tandem Press join us at the Lofts in the near future. If you have not visited the Art Lofts, please attend a gallery opening or stop by for a walk-through.

The exhibition committee—myself, Paul Sacaridiz, Michael Connors, and Elaine Scheer—worked closely with museum director Russell Panczenko, editor Susan Day, exhibitions coordinator Mary Ann Fitzgerald, and the amazing Jerl Richmond, the chief preparator, who so thoughtfully and meticulously laid out the exhibition. Anne Lambert, curator of education, has arranged for many of the art faculty to lecture during the exhibition.

We hope you enjoy *Compendium 2012*, the catalogue, and the gallery talks.

Tom Loeser
Chair, Art Department

2012 Exhibition of the Faculty of Art at the University of Wisconsin–Madison

A STUDY GUIDE

by Michael Jay McClure, Ph.D.

1) Count the exhibitions

Here you have a catalogue that documents an exhibition. As such, it stands both as proxy for that exhibition and curiously independent from it. If you happen to be reading this within the exhibition space, you can compare the difference between the two. If, as is more likely, you read this in another place, after you have seen the exhibition, before viewing, or without seeing it at all, you will have to trust that the flattened works pictured herein have stood as dimensional, found themselves blanched or made brilliant by the museum lights, and worked with the scale and features of the building that housed them—along with a network of arranged objects, performances, and video events. In other words: once upon a time there was exhibition and now there is a catalogue.

Questions:

This catalogue outlasts the exhibition but necessarily stands in impoverished relationship to it as a spatial, scopic, and social phenomenon. What can we make of that?

What if we said there are two exhibitions here, tethered together with common artists and images: the "actual" exhibition, and the exhibition in the book? What kind of experience would each offer up?

How may art work, or work against, its physical situation? How do we see it in league with staircases, atria, blocks of visitors, occluded views, and wheeling and seasonal light? How do we relate to art in a book like this?

2) Check Yourself

In most histories of art, the spectator remains generic and theoretical. We imagine a general viewer in front of a discrete piece of art. One of the hallmarks of the contemporary, however, might be that this spectator, whom we have only generally imagined, becomes central to the work of art. We might also acknowledge that the piece of art has shattered into *pieces*. With serial art, for instance, the viewer might be charged with tracing out the schematic formula that produced multiple objects across an exhibit; in an installation, one might be courted as a sentient and sensorial being; in conceptual art one might see the gap between data and what it would describe. In this exhibition, the media proliferate. We witness photography, sculpture, painting, video, installation, performance, and *whatever*. However, if the spectator takes a central position in contemporary art, does it not stand to reason that he or she is a medium, and a material, within it? In other words, you are not general, even if this writer cannot imagine you specifically. Thus, how do you matter in this artwork? Let us think about that.

3) Museum Fever

Here is a puzzle. While this show promises to be snapshot of the contemporary, upon exhibition the contemporary becomes a finished phenomenon, part of a visual archive, and thus part of a past. Moreover, it becomes *organized*. Part of this organizational apparatus is literal and visible: this art is housed within the Chazen Museum of Art, and specifically in its newly doubled and soaring spaces. Moreover, part of the organizational apparatus that shapes the exhibition remains unseen, but manifest: expectations of the curators, limitations of space, departmental expectations, academic concerns, and the relentlessness of deadlines all define this show to a certain degree. But beyond that other, philosophical, apparatuses do their work. For instance, art becomes visible as art because the artist and spectator recognize it as such. Further, we can imagine other, intertwined critical discourses clamping down, for instance: the privileging of certain types of expression, the belief or rejection of expression itself, the definition of the "contemporary," and the filters of Art History. Education does its work here, as does economics, as does privilege. If we define the museum as the institution that organizes art, its structure extends beyond the physical. Living and staffed, attended and edited, cleaned and administered, disciplined and conserving, the museum structure asserts itself in manifold ways.

4) Mirror Reverse

Excuse a brief *discursus*. The mirror has long been an inveigling and frustrating reflecting device. Its images do not last and it meets its objects in reverse: right becomes left; letters appear "backwards" in its silver demesne. Of course, some of the most formidable thinkers, psychoanalysts, philosophers, writers, storytellers, anthropologists, mythmakers, and poets have mused upon this uncanny replicator. Their analysis seems especially piqued when bodies appear and reverse themselves when mirrored. They note that figures seem to coalesce and become strange. Of course, any reflection, literal and no, is bound to misapproximate, to reverse and frame, in ways that limit the subject. Let us see this exhibition as a reflection, if not of the artists, then of those who participate in art, or if not just that, then a picture of the social humanscape. Approximated bodies stand in these frames and bodies made them. As an example and reflection, then, of a social network, this "mirror" distorts and circumvents. The ways it does so should compel its viewers.

Questions:

Who is reflected and suggested here? Who is missing?

Are there figures haunting this exhibition that are particular to "our time?"

In these representations of the human—who appear in indexical, iconic, and symbolic ways—can we imagine beings, or ways of being, that resist definition?

5) Subjunctive Cases

As an art historian, I have been interested in a certain critical category that appears within grammar, but does not find an equivalent within visual analysis. That would be the subjunctive case, or language that expresses a wish, makes a hypothesis, allows something, or works in other counterfactual ways. Examples include "God save the Queen!" "That I was in the wide and laneless sea" and "I would that it were so." Indeed, the subjunctive fascinates because it allows language to not be merely reflective (the mirror returns) or representational,

but suggestive. I would like to think that certain images, as visual signs, work in the same way. After all, this art establishes a certain grammatical, social, and meaningful context, thus a powerful visual proposal, or a certain suggested *irreality*, could exist here as well. However, this subjunctive case, or mood, would work in terms that are visual or otherwise artistic.

Question:

What is the wish, or what are the wishes, within this exhibition?

6) Fun Facts

"Artful" means cunning, not artistic; the same could be said of "crafty."

Visual and formal analysis is usually thought to be a written exercise. This obscures a type of criticality that can be located in art objects, or artwork, already.

An upright, reversible mirror on a stand is called a psyche.

This started as an essay on the changing interactive spaces of contemporary art. Then I decided to make an interactive space through language.

matthew
bakkom

Assistant Professor
UW–Madison Department of Art, since 2011
Photography

2007 Master of Fine Arts, University
of Minnesota

1999 Studio program, Whitney Museum
Independent Study Program

1993 Film certificate, Film in the Cities

1991 Bachelor of Arts, University
of Virginia

The creative interpretation of archives often serves as the basis for my work. This activity is grounded in an expanded notion of photographic and sculptural practice. My approach emphasizes concept, materials, and methods of assemblage alongside the use of appropriate tools for the pursuit and presentation of complex ideas such as intimacy, complaint, justice, and power. The intention throughout is to "animate" the archival material in the service of the super-structural concept, resulting in gestures that are ultimately resolved in the organization of matter, time, and space. As visual artists of the past harnessed cultural allegory through the shaping of stone, bronze, wood, pigment, and canvas, I draw on the vast field of historical image objects that silently underpin our culture, bringing them to a new light, transformed by novel production methods and combinatory aesthetic strategies.

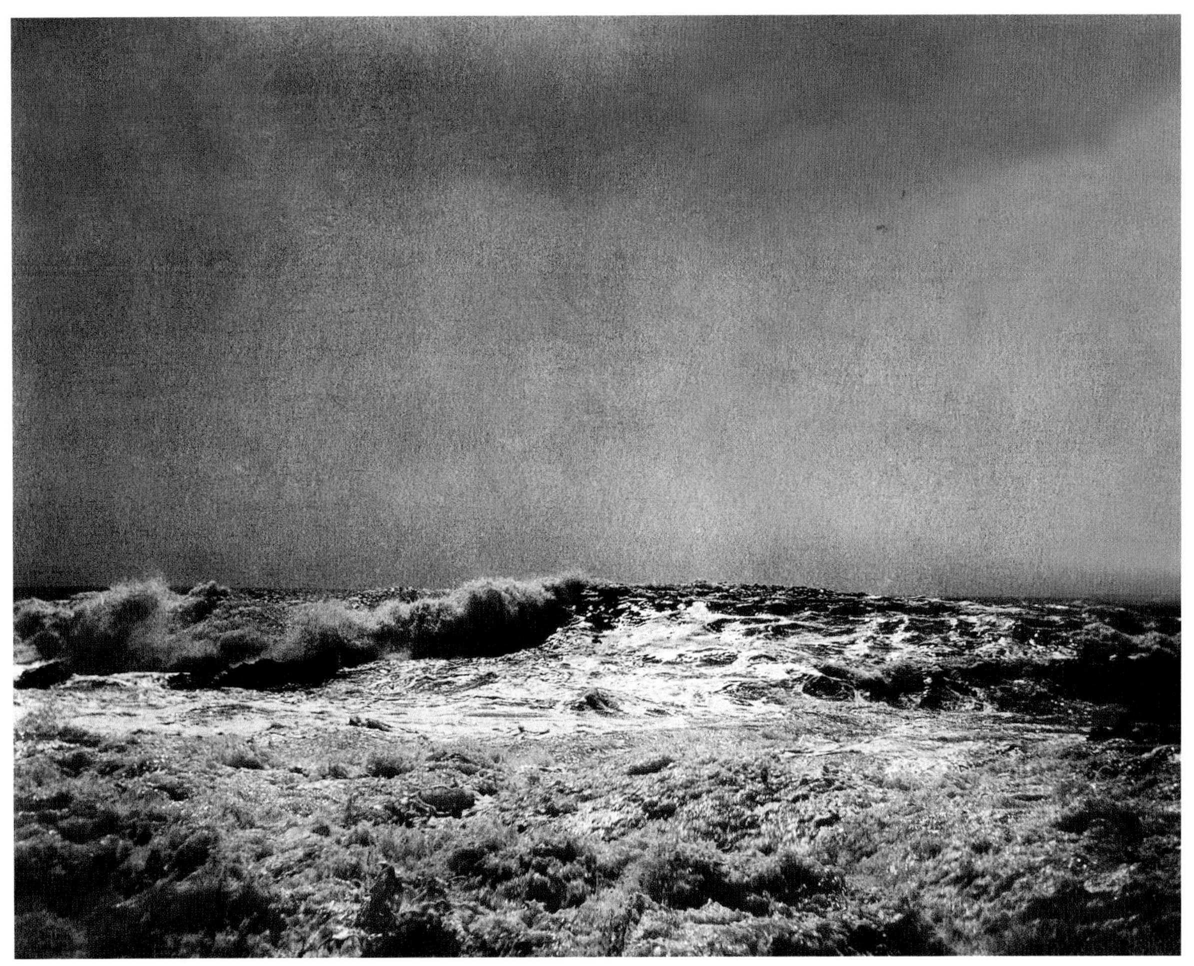

Recent career achievements

2011 *The Invisible Hand of Jules Maciet*, Biblioteque Des Musee des Arts Decoratif exhibition, Paris, France

2010 *Some Scientific Expeditions*, Bell Museum of Natural History exhibition, Minneapolis, Minn.

2010–2011 Mcknight Foundation Visual Arts Fellow

2010 3-month residency at the Recollet International Exchange and Accommodation Center, Paris, France

2009 *New York City Museum of Complaint* (Göttingen: Steidl-Miles)

2008–2009 Bush Foundation Visual Arts Fellow

Works in exhibition

Day for Night, 2011, ink on canvas, 36 x 48 in. (illustrated)

Loveless, 2011, ink on canvas, 23 x 20 in.

derrick l.
buisch

Professor
UW–Madison Department of Art, since 1997
Painting, Drawing

1996 Master of Fine Arts, University of
Minnesota, Minneapolis

1995 Skowhegan School of Painting and
Sculpture, Skowhegan, Maine

1989 Bachelor of Fine Arts, Maryland
Institute College of Art

"I believe in maps, diagrams, codes, chess-games, puzzles, airline timetables, airport indicator signs."

—J.G. Ballard

I am interested in painting impossible places. My hope is to evoke spaces that are familiar but exist right on the edge of tangibility. Notational activities in the studio and workbooks include indexing, listing, charting, and graphing—all to create numerous ways to build visually dense paintings that employ layered references in varied compositions.

The paintings mean to look like a collision of visual information—a mix-up of signs, symbols, letters, words, fragments, parts, and pieces of pictures, all operating with a hyperactivity to evoke an optically charged field. A calculated tension with the figure ground relationships reconciles random bits and pieces of visual information into a resonant rebus.

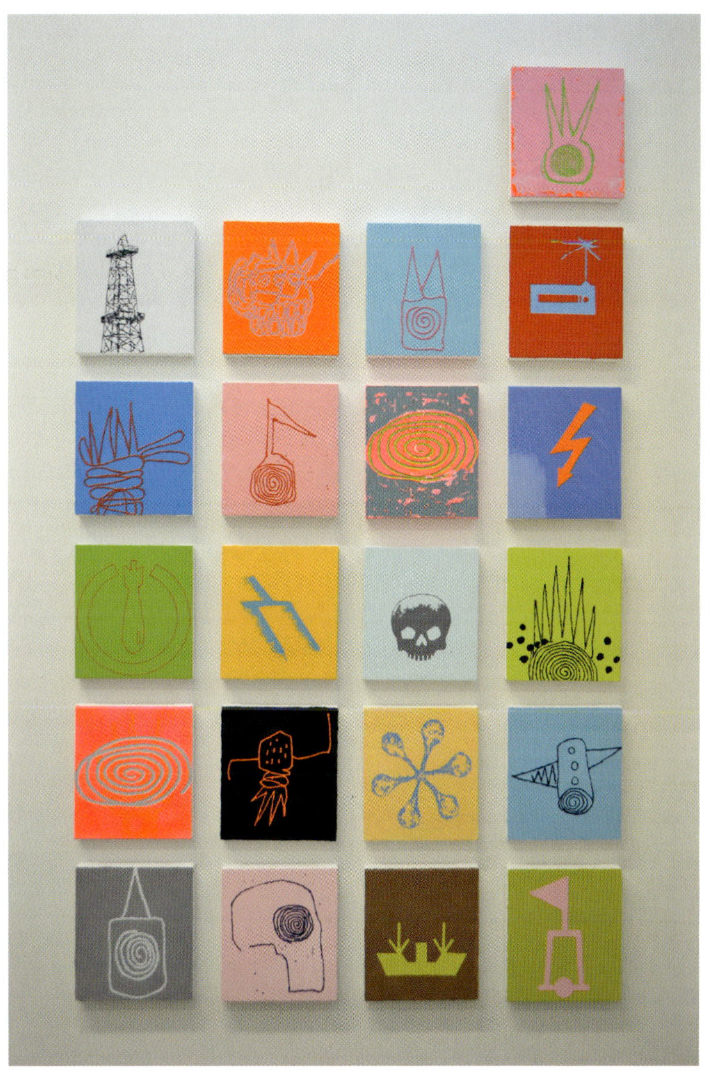

Recent career achievements

2011 *Vermilion Sands +*, solo exhibition at James Watrous Gallery, Madison, Wisc.

2011 *COLOR VIBRATIONS, SUMMER IN WISCONSIN*, Tory Folliard Gallery group exhibition, Milwaukee, Wisc.

2010 *Wisconsin Triennial*, Madison Museum of Contemporary Art group exhibition, Madison, Wisc.

2009 *Drift*, Edenfred solo exhibition, Madison, Wisc.

2006 *Pink Flag*, JEMA, UICA solo exhibition, Grand Rapids, Mich.

2003 *News from the Sun*, Mississippi State University solo exhibition

2001 *ooomph*, Klein Art Works group exhibition, Chicago, Ill.

2000 Pollock-Krasner Foundation Grant, New York City, N.Y.

Works in exhibition

ERRATA INDEX 21, 2011, mixed media on canvas over panel, 21 pieces, each 12 x 11 in. (illustrated; image courtesy Tory Folliard Gallery)

The Kingdom of Yellow, 2010–11, oil and acrylic on canvas, 72 x 96 in.

Studio Notations, 2011, paint, silkscreen, collage, mixed media on six boxes, 16-in. cubes, wood, variable installation dimensions.

laurie beth
clark

Professor

UW–Madison Department of Art, since 1985

Video, Performance, Installation, Visual Culture Studies, Relational Aesthetics

1983 Master of Fine Arts, Rutgers University

1981 Master of Arts, University of New Mexico

1976 Bachelor of Arts, Hampshire College

os•su•ar•y (osh-oo-er-ee) noun: repository of bones, from Latin, first known use 1658

This exhibition inaugurates *Ossuary*, for which I have invited hundreds of artists to create a single bone or a cluster of bones, in any medium, in two, three, or four dimensions. The contributions are political statements and personal elegies, memorials to individuals and statements about mortality. They may represent connections to our ancestors or to our descendants. Some are serious and others completely playful.

Ossuary was inspired by the repositories of bones that have accrued in countries like Cambodia and Rwanda where mass violence has taken place. But *Ossuary* is not a project about those traumas; rather, I believe that artists counter images of pain with hopeful or poignant rejoinders. Envisioning hope for the world is one of the things that art can do.

Contributions to the Chazen display were received before 2012, but *Ossuary* is an ongoing project. Details about artists and participation are at www.ossuaries.wordpress.com.

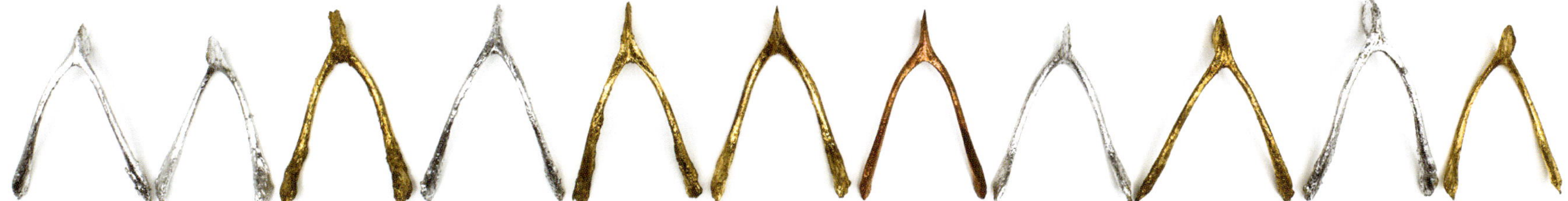

Recent career achievements

2011 *Cafe Allonge*, a Spatula & Barcode performance,
Montreal, Quebec, Canada

2011 *Bicycle Map Spoon*, a Spatula & Barcode performance,
Utrecht, Netherlands

2011 *In/Of the City: Tangier*, a Spatula & Barcode performance, Tangier, Morocco

2011 "Never Again and its Discontents," *Performance
Research: A Journal of the Performing Arts* 16, no. 1: 68–79.

2011 "What the Jews Do," *TDR: The Drama Review* 55 no.
3: 144–152.

Works in exhibition

Ossuary, 2012 (ongoing), mixed media installation
(detail illustrated)

michael
connors

Professor
UW–Madison Department of Art, since 1998
Printmaking

1996 Master of Fine Arts, UW–Madison

1994 Bachelor of Arts, UW–Madison

WATER LOGS explores the crossed connections between science and art as applied to the study of the systems of lakes (limnology) and the study of the soul as expressed in spiritual, psychological, and philosophical systems. The art research question posed is as follows: "Is this lake my soul?" The methodology pursued involves "aesthetic sampling" of the lake to check its qualitative condition—for example, water purity. When water is polluted, is the soul polluted as well? Although fact and mystery remain antagonists, the bigger question for both science and art remains: can humans live in harmony with the constantly threatened natural world? Or is a degraded world indicative of a degraded soul?

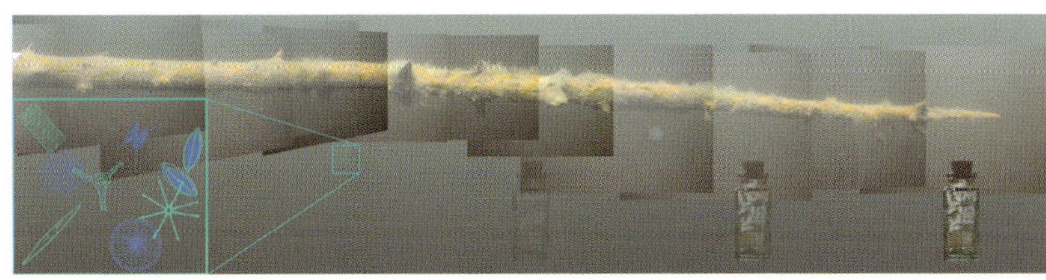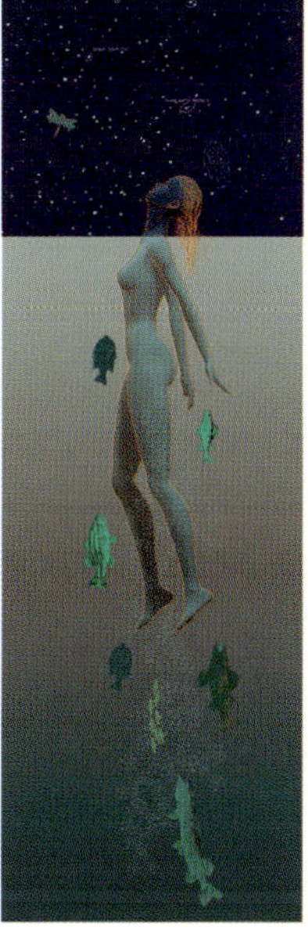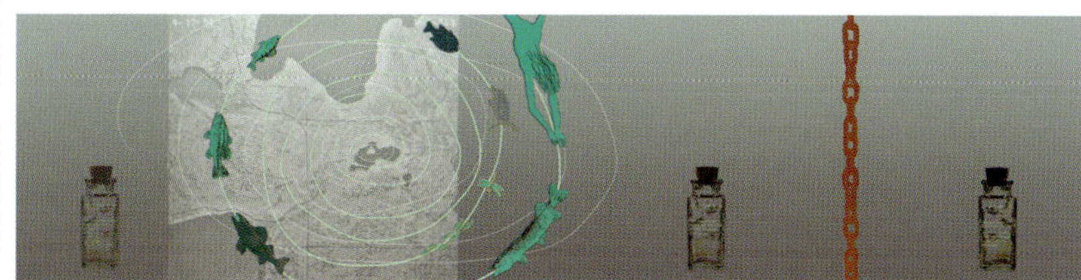

Recent career achievements

2011 *Spacium Tempus: 3rd MAAPS International Printmaking Exhibition*, Alchemy Gallery, Beijing, China and Guanlan Original Printmaking Base, Shenzhen, China

2011 *Paper in Particular National Exhibition*, Columbia College, Columbia, Mo.

2011 *Library Thoughts*, Raday Konyveshaz Gallery, Budapest, Hungary

2009 *Los Angeles Printmaking Society 20th National Exhibition*, Los Angeles Municipal Art Gallery, Los Angeles, Calif.

2009 *32nd Bradley International Print and Drawing Exhibition*, Heuser Art Center, Bradley University, Peoria, Ill.

2009 *Identity: Unlimited Editions*, Craft and Folk Art Museum, Los Angeles, Calif.

2008 *One World, Invitational International Print Exhibition*, Cultural Olympics Festivities, Beijing, China

Works in exhibition

WATER LOGS (triptych), 2010, archival inkjet, polyester plate lithograph, relief, colored pencil, and pastel on inkjet coated 100 percent cotton rag paper, 72 x 202 in. (illustrated)

kim
cridler

Associate Professor
UW–Madison Department of Art, since 2005
Metals

1993 Master of Fine Arts, State University of
New York at New Paltz

1989 Bachelor of Fine Arts, University of
Michigan–Ann Arbor

I am an object maker. I love objects and believe in their power to record and extend our lives. My practice is to create a body of work that activates an awareness of the world of making and using, recognizes the humanity that resides in the act of containment and collection, champions ornamentation and the potential of beauty, and acknowledges the irreducible power of material and form when skillfully and meaningfully employed.

One way I frame my interests is through the vessel. Urn and vase forms are icons of continuity and reminders of the world of making and using. They symbolize collection and preservation, as well as ceremony and abundance. My current work links considerations of form and ornament with an investigation of my environment through a collection of vessels in shelving units, referencing museum storage areas that facilitate the formal and cultural study of objects. The vessels' spare structures are ornamented based on studies made during my practice of collecting plant and insect life from the fields around my home.

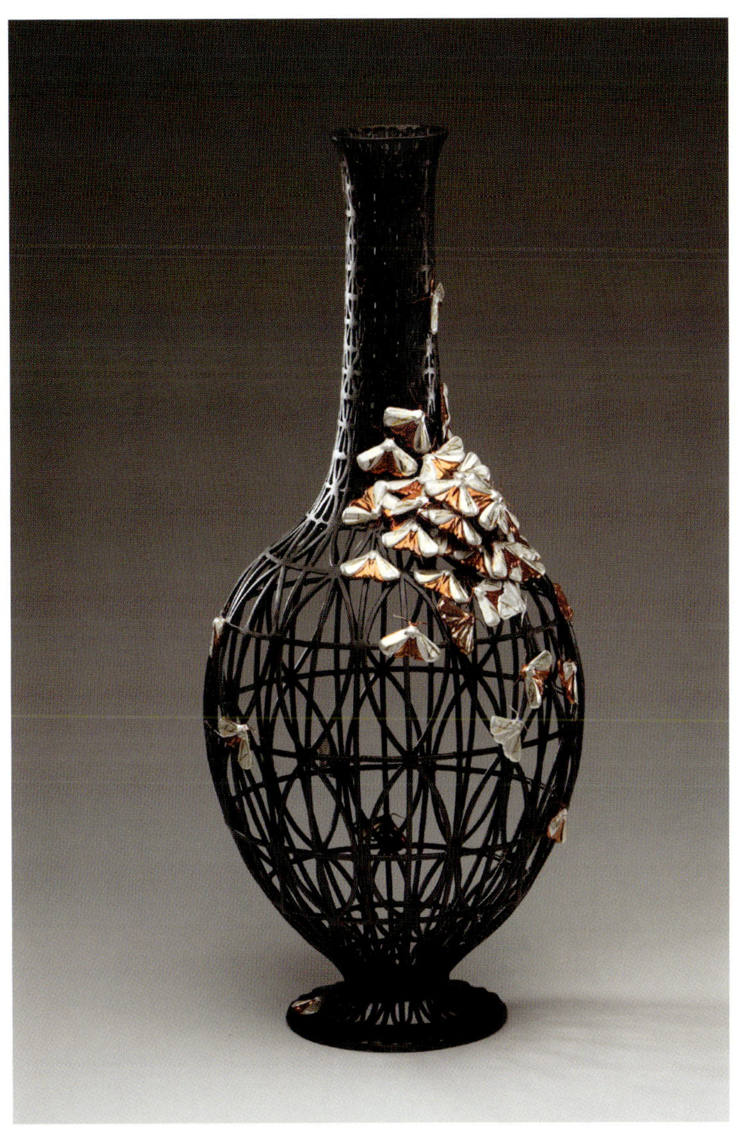

Recent career achievements

2013 *Kim Cridler: Tributaries*, National Ornamental Metal Museum solo exhibition, Memphis, Tenn.

2012 *Kim Cridler*, Lisa Sette Gallery solo exhibition, Scottsdale, Ariz.

2011 *Kim Cridler: My Wisconsin Home*, Racine Art Museum solo exhibition, Racine, Wisc.

2011 *Arbor Alma*, UW–Oshkosh Sage Hall public art commission

2009/2010 Vilas Associates Award, the Graduate School, UW–Madison

2004 Wisconsin Arts Board Visual Arts Fellowship

Works in exhibition

Untitled (Case), 2011, steel, bronze, silver, glass, 72 x 32 x 30 in.

Field Study #2, 2010, steel, copper, silver, gold, 28 x 13 in.

Photo: Jim Escalante (illustrated; not in exhibition)

jack
damer

Professor
UW–Madison Department of Art, since 1970
Printmaking

1965 Master of Fine Arts, Carnegie
Mellon University

1960 Bachelor of Arts, Carnegie
Mellon University

My work in this exhibition is a compilation of previous graphic interests utilizing traditional printmaking, drawing, photography, and, more recently, digital formats. It is a relationship between imagery and formal invention. It also celebrates the act of making and hands-on production including an investigation into processes that lend themselves to extensive reworking and variation. Accordingly, the work is layered with subtle and ambiguous meaning that commemorates the ritual beauty and discipline associated with graphic production.

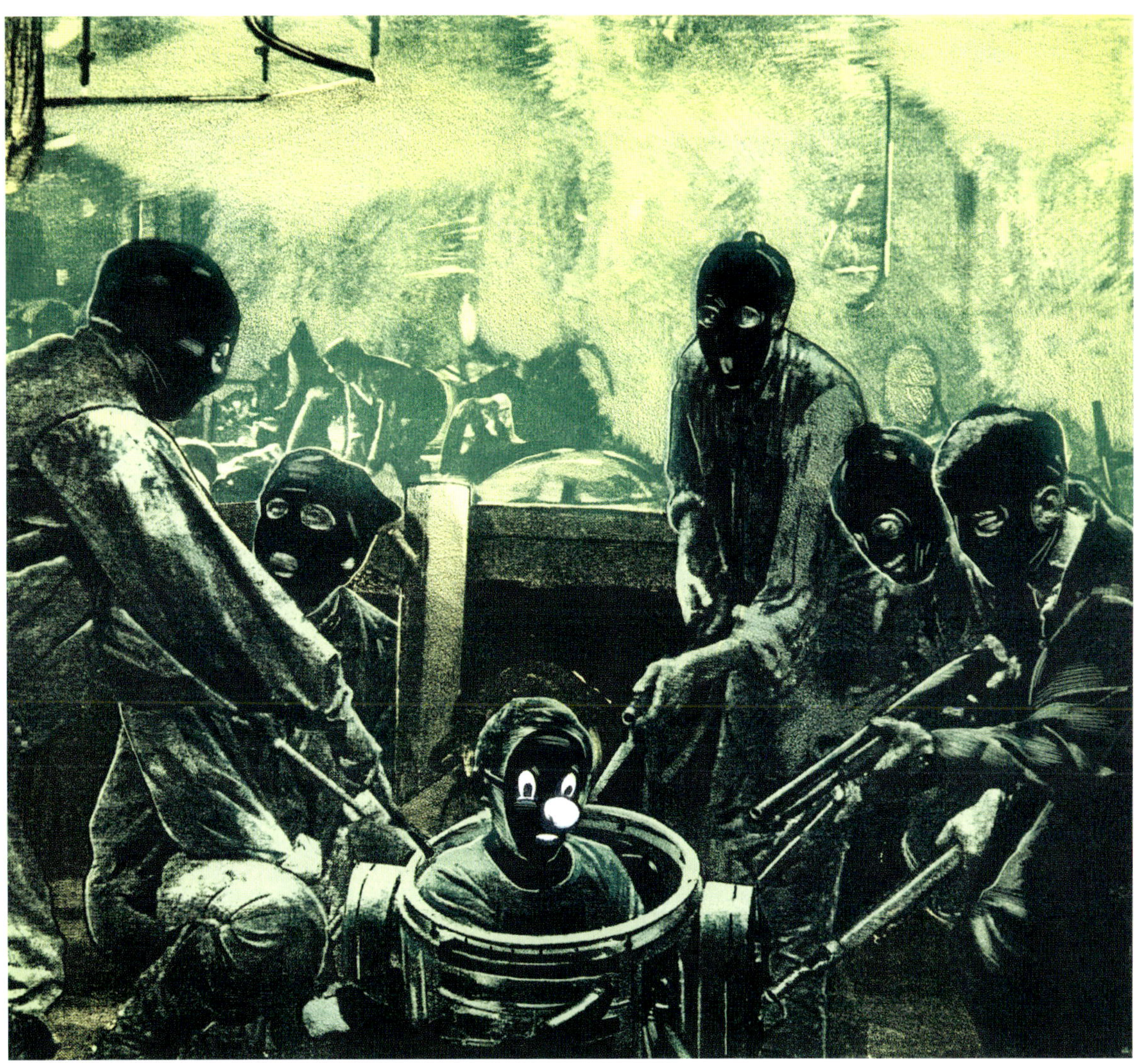

Recent career achievements

2011 *Tempting Equilibrium* SGC International Juried
Exhibition, Des Lee Gallery, St. Louis, Mo.

2010 *Print Summit*, Wellington Gray Gallery, University
of North Carolina

2009 *Impact 6*, "Old Traditions / New Clothes,"
University of West England

2010 *Prints USA*, Springfield Art Museum,
Springfield, Mo.

Works in exhibition

Wall and floor installation comprising graphic objects
and mixed media prints

Death of Whimsy, 2011, lithograph, 13 1/2 x 15 in.
(illustrated; not in exhibition)

jim a.
escalante

Professor
UW–Madison, Department of Art, since 1989
Graphics

1981 Master of Fine Arts, UW–Madison

1977 Ecole Regionale des Beaux-Arts et des Arts Appliques, Reims, France

1976 Bachelor of Fine Arts, North Texas State University

Photography and book arts are my greatest interests. As technology becomes more integrated in our daily life, I search for new ways to reflect on our history and our craft. Taking photographs of books is one way that I immerse myself in the art and craft that feeds my soul. The other is by collaborating with artists, writers, and students. It is the most rewarding way to learn and to explore.

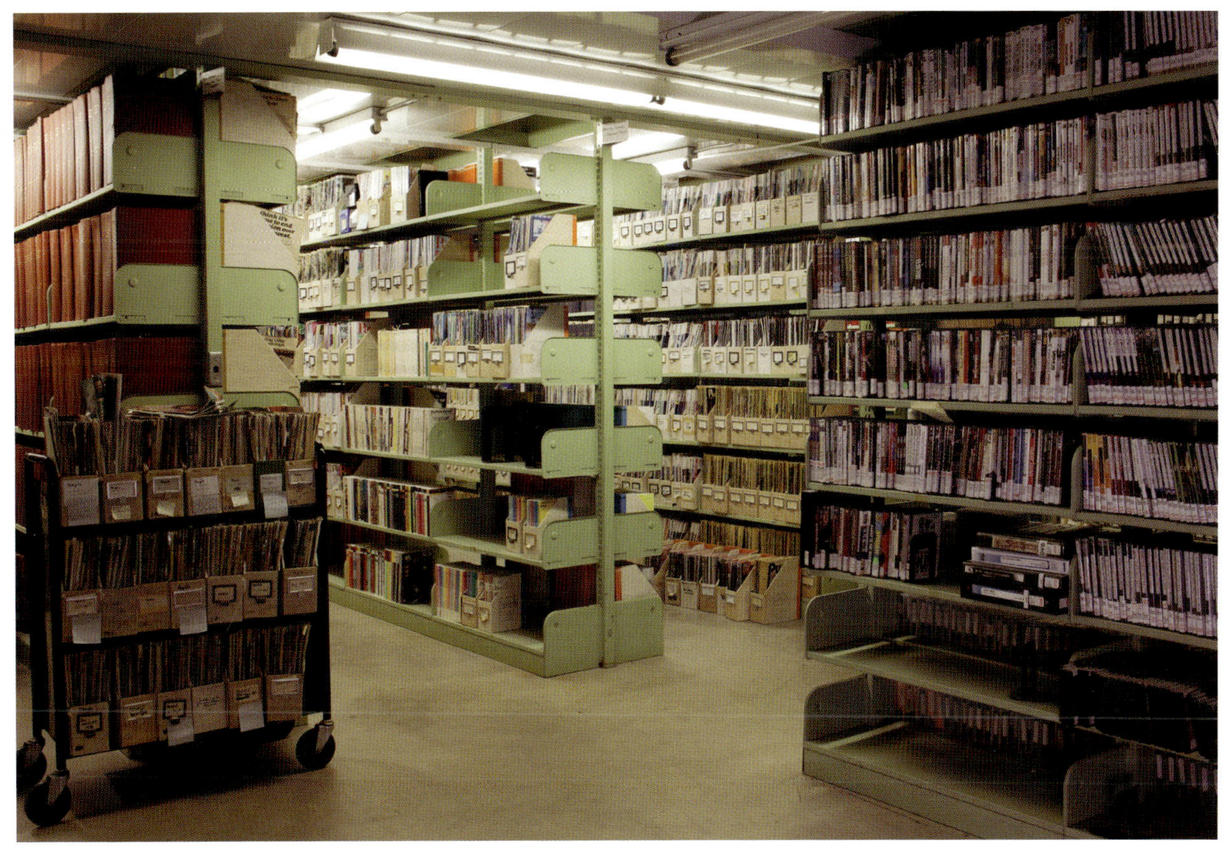

Recent career achievements

2010–2011 Designer for *Hand Papermaking*, 24 no. 2, 25 no.1, 25 no. 2

2010 Photographer for *Lisa Gralnick: The Gold Standard*, Bellevue Arts Museum, Bellevue, Wash.

Works in exhibition

20110904 Madison Public Library 0093, 2011, inkjet photographic print, 16 x 20 in.

201011112 Madison Public Library 9785, 2011, inkjet photographic print, 16 x 20 in. (illustrated)

steve
feren

Professor
UW–Madison Department of Art, since 1983
Glass

1981 Master of Fine Arts, Rutgers University

1979 Bachelor of Fine Arts, Alfred University

1971 Dayton Art Institute

"The eye was made by the light, for the light, so that the inner light may emerge to meet the outer light.

"MEPHISTOPHELES: Freely, I admit it, I have hardly done a thing—If you compare this idiotic world of 'Somethingness' with that other world of 'Nothingness'! I had not realized how nearly futile were my efforts! I sent tidal waves and storms and earthquakes, holocausts—when all was done, the sea and land remained as quiet as before. And as for that accursed trash, that progeny of animals and men, there is absolutely nothing I can do with them! How many of them have I so far buried in the earth! Yet fresh new blood is always circulating! On and on it goes! I should be driven mad! Seeds by the thousands, bursting forth from Air, from Water, even Earth, Dry! Moist! Warm! Cold! If I had not reserved the element of Fire for myself, I would not have a thing to call my own."—Goethe, *Faust*

My work is concerned with the persistence of life and the miracle of discovery and creation. This all is given voice through the physical/nonphysical phenomenon of light.

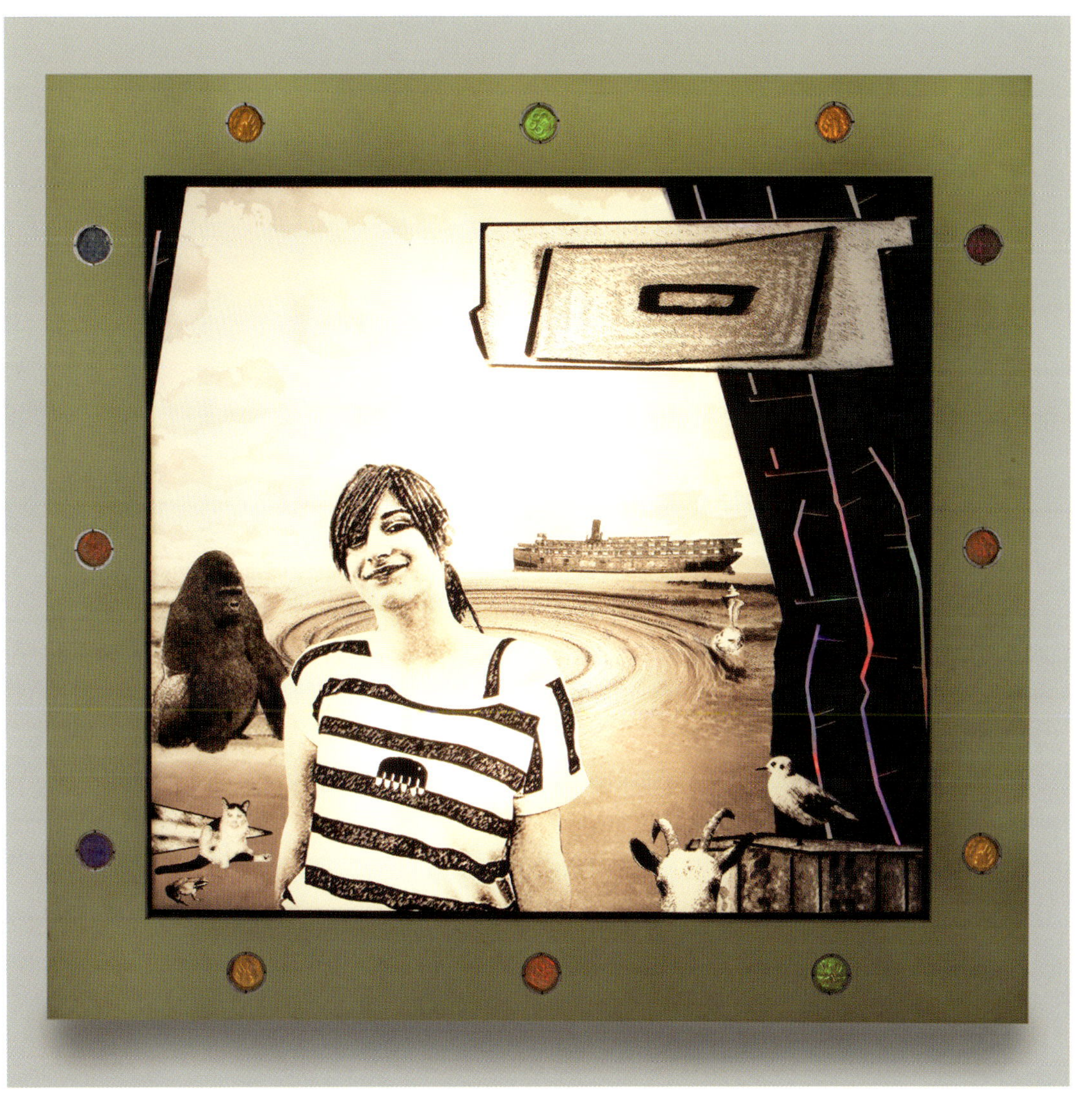

Recent career achievements

2011 Entrance for new performing arts center, UW–Parkside

2011 *Sources*, cast glass gates for city library, Fitchburg, Wisc.

2009 Kohl Center Promenade commission, Madison, Wisc., collaboration with Gail Simpson

2007 Riverside Medical Clinic, informational light sculpture, Riverside, Calif.

2006 Milwaukee River Arches, Milwaukee, Wisc.

Works in exhibition

The incredible beingness of light 1 (moose), 2011, glass, light, concrete, 5 ft. x 72 in. x 32 in.

The incredible beingness of light 2 (gorilla), 2011 glass, light, concrete, 9 x 6 ft. Diam.

The incredible beingness of light 3 (groundhog), 2011 glass, light, concrete, 68 x 48 in. Diam.

Zoralita, 2009, glass, wood, acrylic print, light, 55 x 59 x 5 in. (illustrated; not in exhibition)

sarah
fitzsimons

Assistant Professor
UW–Madison Department of Art, since 2011
Sculpture

2005 Master of Fine Arts, University of
California, Los Angeles

2000 Bachelor of Fine Arts, Ohio University,
Athens, Ohio

2000 Bachelor of Arts, Ohio University,
Athens, Ohio

My projects typically involve an outdoor sculpture that interacts with and derives meaning from its surroundings. I interpret this process with photographs and video, sometimes reconfiguring and presenting the images as separate pieces.

In September, 2010, I was invited to build a piece on the island of Mandø in western Denmark. Mandø is a starkly beautiful, isolated place, with a harsh climate and swiftly changing weather. It is often cut off from the mainland by the tide, with no ferry service, no airport, and no bridge.

Initially, I carried my work to the island in a backpack. The first day I built a house on a high dune overlooking the town and sea. Each day I redesigned and redrew the structure, moving it downhill until I reached the shore by the end of the week. On the vast tidal flats, the house flooded twice a day: the sea entered through doors and walls, with no barriers to keep out the weather.

This house did not offer shelter or privacy, warmth, security, or permanence. It was a structure without roof, walls, or floor—only minimal lines to define the space of a house within the greater expanse of the landscape.

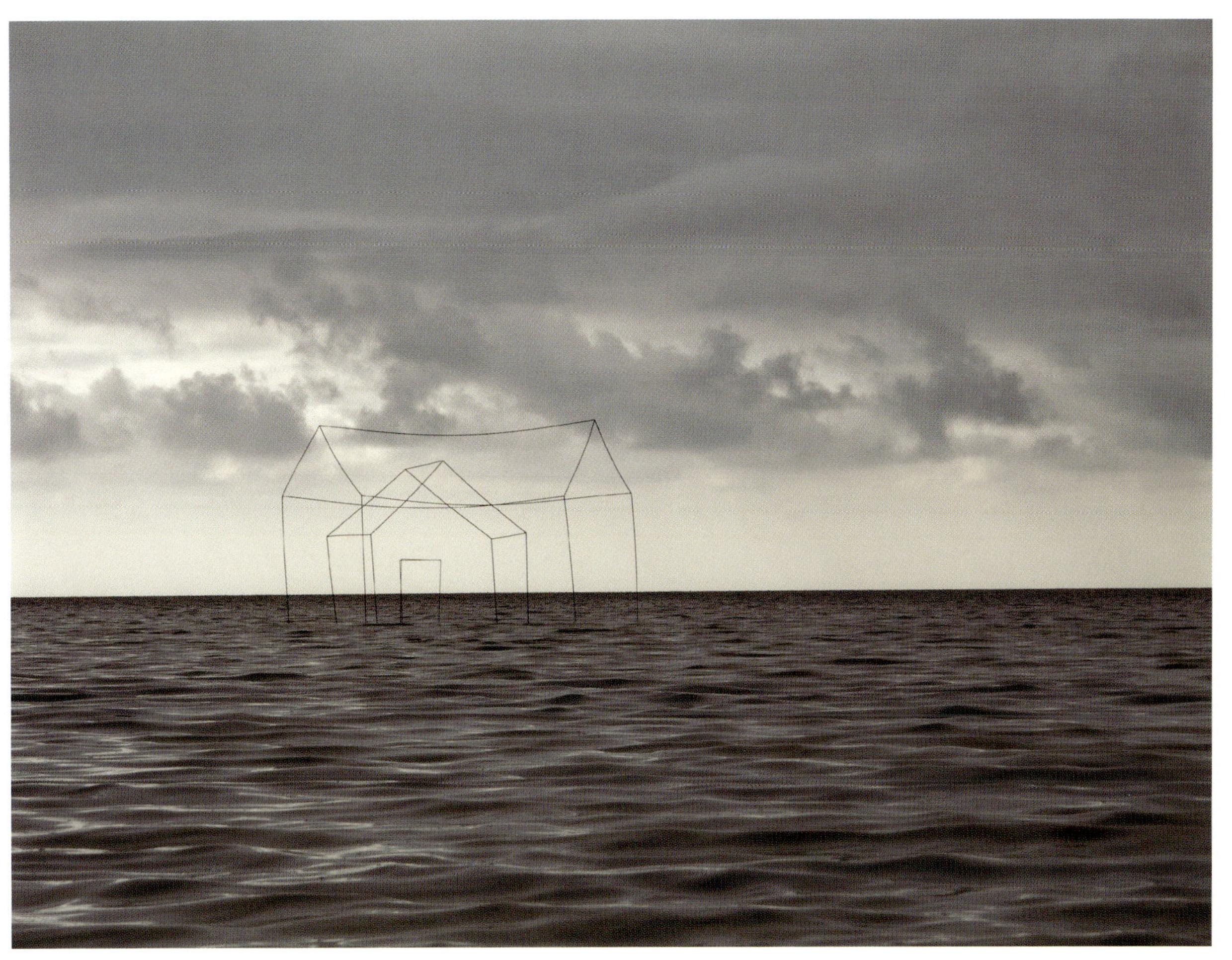

Recent career achievements

2010 *Any Questions? – the Mandø Dialogues*, exhibition and 10-day residency in Mandø, Denmark, for the Wadden Sea Festival

2009 MacDowell Colony Fellowship, Peterborough, N.H.

2009 I-Park Environmental Art Biennale and Residency, East Haddam, Conn.

2008 *Fusion Culture*, SoFA Gallery solo exhibition, Indiana University, Bloomington

2007 *Orogeny*, EnView Gallery solo exhibition, Long Beach, Calif.

2005 *Supersonic*, Pacific Design Center group exhibition, Los Angeles, Calif.

Works in exhibition

Photos of *House for Mandø, Denmark*, 2010, aluminum, island, and sea. Standard configuration: 35 x 30 x 20 ft. Wadden Sea covers approx 6,017 sq. mi. Photos: 30 x 48 in.

aristotle
georgiades

Professor
UW–Madison Department of Art, since 1999
Sculpture

1984 Master of Fine Arts, School of the Art
Institute of Chicago

1981 Bachelor of Fine Arts, University of
Michigan–Ann Arbor

I work on individual projects and public art as part of *Actual Size*, a collaborative team. In my studio practice some of the objects incorporate material that has been salvaged from one life and given another. Often I use existing objects and repurpose them into expressive sculptural forms. Most of these sculptures make reference to our continuous desire to move through life with purpose. I see these repurposed objects as a metaphor for our human need to adapt and change directions when confronted with obstacles or failures.

The themes of labor and the changing role of the worker in society have permeated my work throughout my career. The recent economic crisis has presented a different way of looking at these issues and new opportunities to explore them. This country's economy and much of the world's has changed forever. People's ideas of success and achieving goals have changed. More modest ideals seem to be common and one must be prepared to find alternative means to an end.

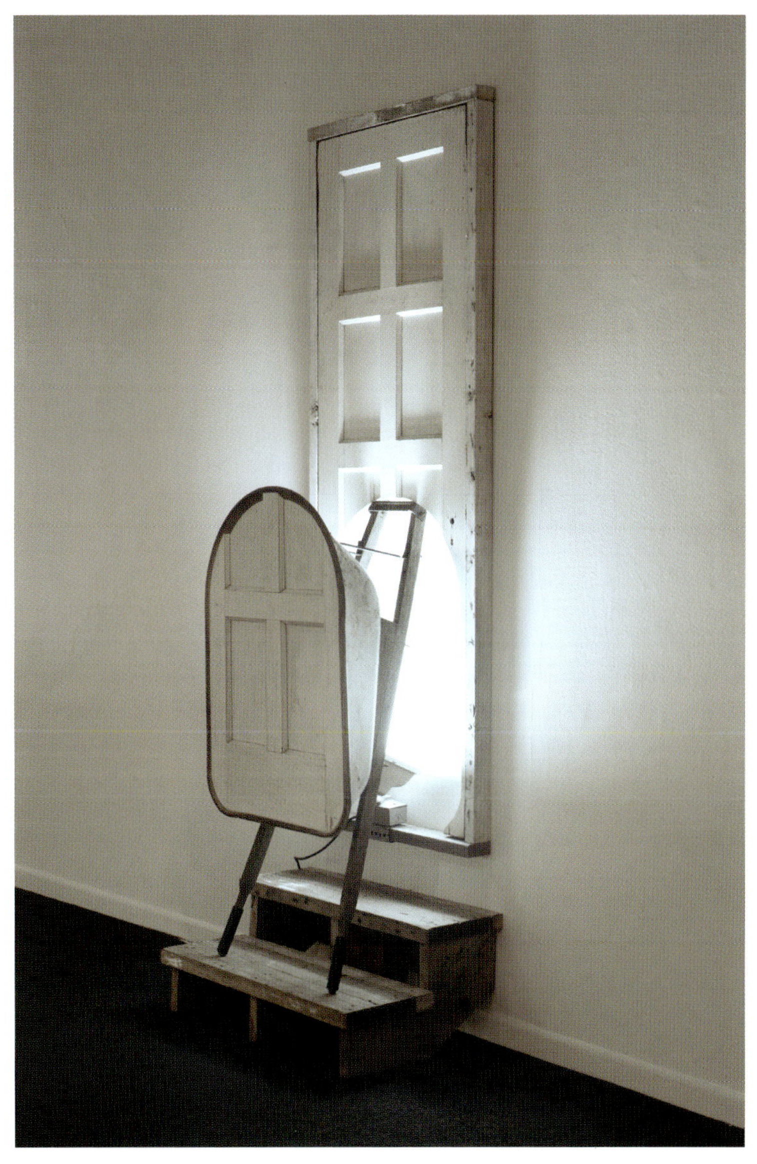

Recent career achievements

2011 *Repurposed*, Chicago Cultural Center solo
exhibition, Chicago, Ill.

2011 *Gift*, Nature Unframed temporary public art project
at Morton Arboretum, Lisle, Ill. (as part of *Actual Size*)

2010 *Woodness*, Unsmoke Gallery, Braddock, Penn.

2010 Best in show, *2010 Outdoor Sculpture Exhibit*,
Cary, N.C. (as part of *Actual Size*)

2009 Public art commission, Warch Student Center,
Lawrence University, Appleton, Wisc. (as part of
Actual Size)

2009 *Accidentally On Purpose*, Wriston Art Gallery solo
exhibition, Lawrence, University, Appleton, Wisc.

2007 *Construct*, installation at Baltimore Sculpture
Project, Baltimore, Md.

Works in exhibition

Wrinkle, 2009, 18 ft. x 24 in. x 32 in., aluminum ladder
Homestead, 2011, wood, door, wheelbarrow, light,
96 x 36 x 24 in. (illustrated)

lisa
gralnick

Professor
UW–Madison Department of Art, since 2001
Metals

1980 Master of Fine Arts, State University
of New York at New Paltz

1977 Bachelor of Fine Arts, Kent State
University

The Prototype and the Image Belong to the Category of Related Things is a transitional, final work in a series titled *The Gold Standard*. Separate from the larger body of work and executed after the series' completion, it is a meaningful harbinger of current and future pursuits. It remains a somber rant against the intellectual reduction-ism that threatens to eradicate the defining ingredients of art and its objecthood.

As I embark on a new body of work that utilizes highly patterned polychrome surfaces in vitreous enamel, I find myself interested in the psycho/sexual language of the baroque; the intersection of the decorative, the sordid, and the visceral that manifests itself as desire; the pathology of beauty and the beauty of pathology; the madness of sensuality and the still greater madness of a life without it.

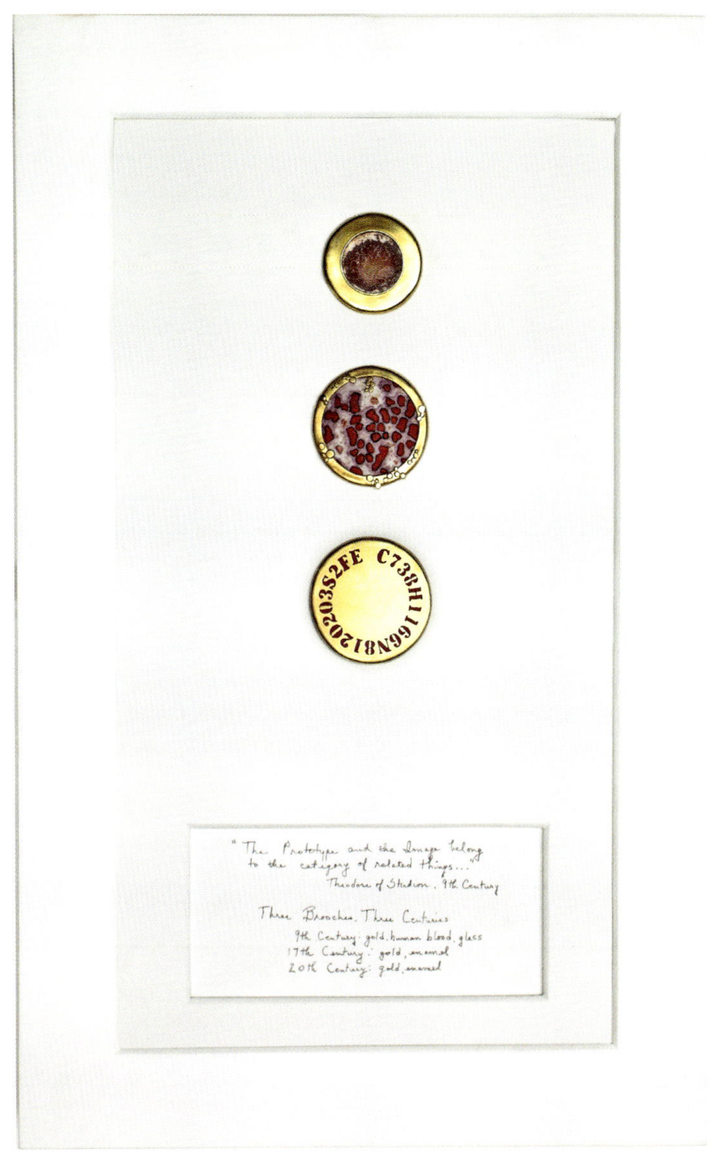

Works in exhibition

Night Blooming Dementia Praecox (four pendants), 2011–12, enamel on copper, sterling silver, gold, pearls, gemstones, handmade chains

Five Brooches, 2011–12, enamel on copper, silver, gemstones

Noble Rot, 2011–12, enamel on copper

The Prototype and the Image Belong to the Category of Related Things, 2011, gold, enamel, human blood, acrylic, 12 x 18 x 1 in. Photo: Jim Escalante (illustrated; not in exhibition)

stephen
hilyard

Associate Professor
UW–Madison Department of Art, since 2004
Computer-Mediated Art

1997 Master of Fine Arts, University of
Southern California, Los Angeles

1989 Master of Arts in architecture,
University of Humberside, U.K.

1983 Bachelor of Arts in architecture,
Edinburgh College of Art, Scotland

Rapture of the Deep consists of eight digitally manipulated landscape images. The series deals with the glamour of risk as personified by eight British mountaineers from the 1970s and '80s, a golden age of high-altitude mountaineering which made many climbers famous. When I was growing up these men were my heroes, and they all died in the mountains. Each piece in the series is named for a climber and the location of his death.

These images were created from photographs I made of underwater landscapes at Silfra, Iceland. The original photographs, made in some of the clearest and coldest water on earth, capture subtly modulated lighting. All other clues to the origins of the images have been removed.

The project title refers to a term coined by Jacques Cousteau to describe the euphoria that divers experience below a certain depth when high-pressure nitrogen dissolved in the body's tissues creates an experience both ecstatic and potentially deadly. The phrase speaks to the nature of sublime experience and the sacrifices demanded of those seek it.

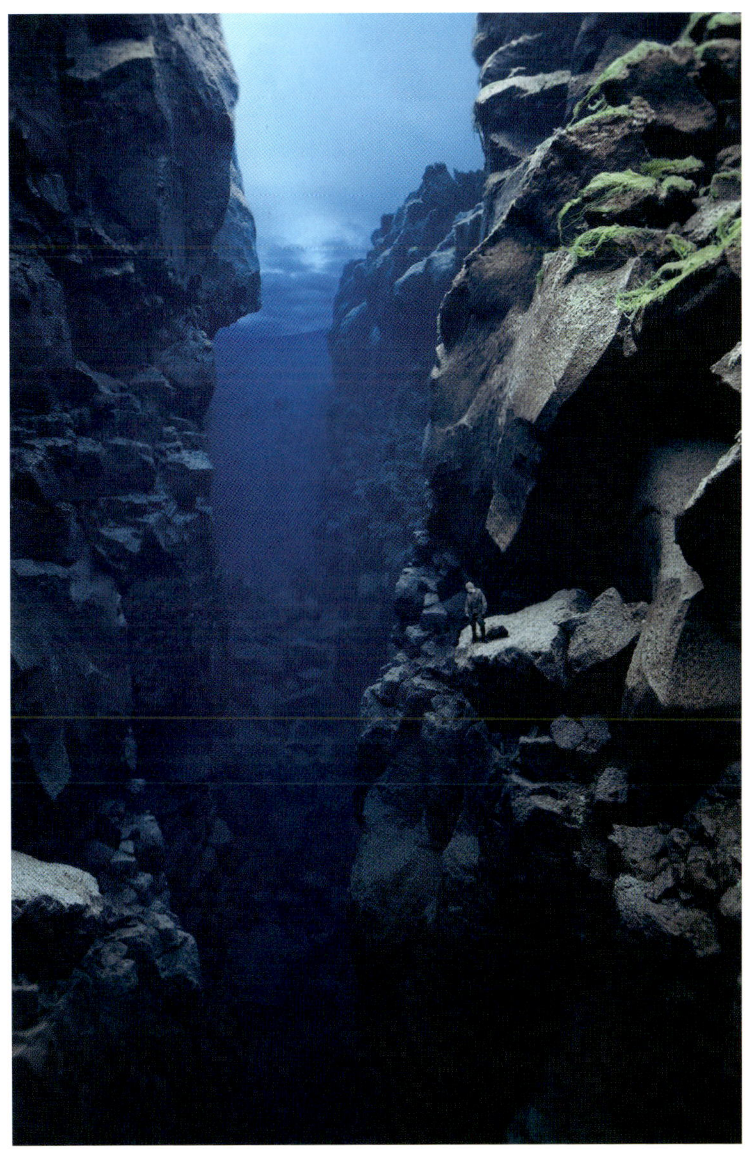

Recent career achievements

2012 *The Arctic Circle Residency*, sailing expedition to the
Spitsbergen Islands

2012 *San Andreas Fellowship: Huntington Library*,
San Marino, Calif.

2011 *Currents 2011 New Media Festival*, Santa Fe, N.M.

2010 *Seven Easy Steps: Artistic Masterpieces*, Horton
Gallery, New York, N.Y.

2009 *Rapture of the Deep*, Platform Gallery, Seattle, Wash.

2008 *The Ends of the Earth*, Five Points Art House,
San Francisco, Calif.

Works in exhibition

Rapture of the Deep (Pete, Everest NE Ridge 1982),
light-jet print in light-box, 29 1/2 x 56 3/4 in.
Rapture of the Deep (Dougal, Leysin 1977), 2009,
light-jet print in light-box, 44 x 29 1/2 in. (illustrated)

john
hitchcock

Professor of Art
UW–Madison Department of Art, since 2001
Relief, Screenprint, Installation

1997 Master of Fine Arts, Texas Tech
University, Lubbock

1990 Bachelor of Fine Arts, Cameron
University, Lawton, Okla.

I use the print medium, with its long history of social and political commentary, to explore relationships of community, land, and culture. My works on paper and multimedia installations consist of prints and moving images that mediate the trauma of war and the fragility of life. Images of U.S. military weaponry are combined with mythological hybrid creatures from the Wichita Mountains of western Oklahoma to explore notions of assimilation and control.

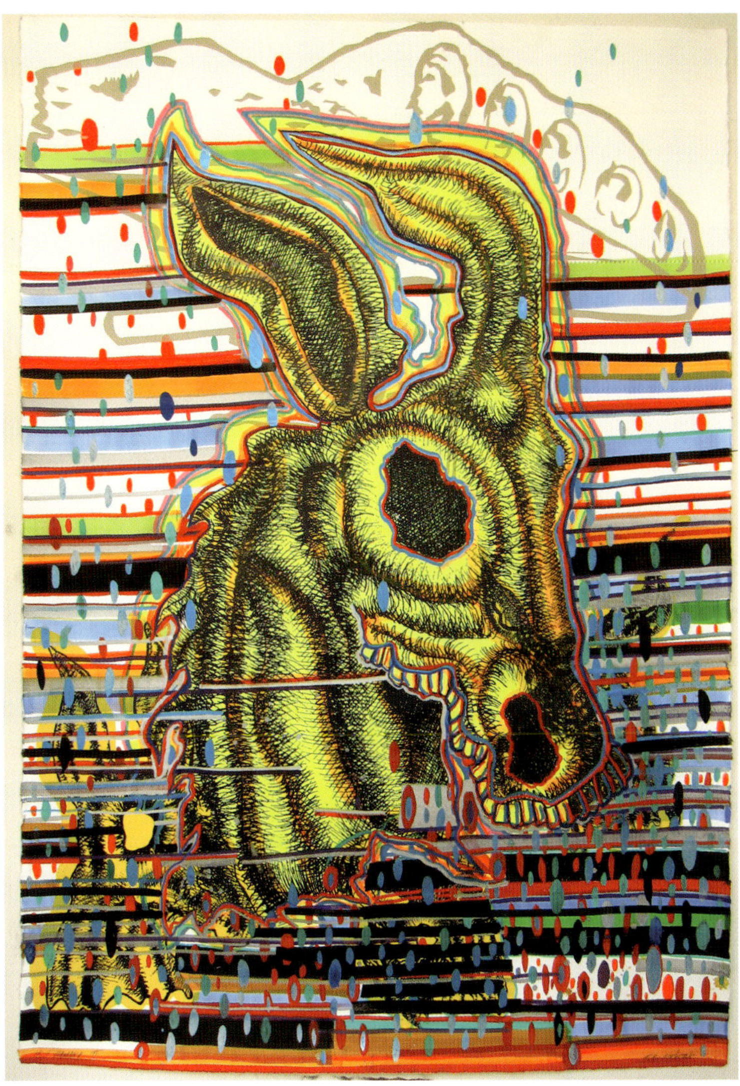

Recent career achievements

2011 Arts Institute Creative Arts Award, UW–Madison

2011 *Epicentro: Re Tracing the Plains,* solo exhibition on the occasion of La Biennale di Venezia 54th International arts exhibition, University of Ca' Foscari, Dipartimento di Studi Linguistici e Culturali Comparati, Venice, Italy

2009 Frans Masereel Centrum for Graphix residency, Kasterlee, Belgium

2008 Expansion Proyecto'ace, International Center for Visual Arts in South America solo exhibition and residency, Buenos Aires, Argentina

2007 *New Prints 2007/Summer–Silkscreen International Print Center New York,* group exhibition, New York, N.Y.

2005–2007 *Changing Hands: Art Without Reservation, Part 2,* The Museum of Arts & Design traveling exhibition, New York, N.Y.

Works in exhibition

Rabbit Hill, 2011, screenprint and ink on paper, 30 x 44 in.

Black Arrow Over the Mountain, 2011, screenprint, ink on paper, 30 x 44 in.

Chemically Wasted (Warhorse), 2011, screenprint, drawing, 30 x 44 in. (illustrated)

Over the Ocean, 2011, screenprint, ink on paper, 30 x 44 in.

Signal Mountain, 2011, screenprint and ink on paper, 30 x 44 in.

s. driscoll
hixson

Assistant Professor
UW–Madison Department of Art, since 2008
Graphic Design

2006 Master of Fine Arts, University of
Michigan–Ann Arbor

1994 Bachelor of Fine Arts, University of
Michigan–Ann Arbor

As my perspectives shift from the vantage point of a motorist to a pedestrian, I witness challenges of navigating every intersection in urban and rural communities.

My work unifies performance and design to spotlight the fragile and fragmented spaces of pedestrian paths. Photo documentation highlights lack of visibility on the crosswalk, while research of traffic signage informs the creation of memorials to pedestrian casualties.

Using design as an expressive form of visual communication, I seek to raise awareness of compromised and limited zones designated for pedestrians.

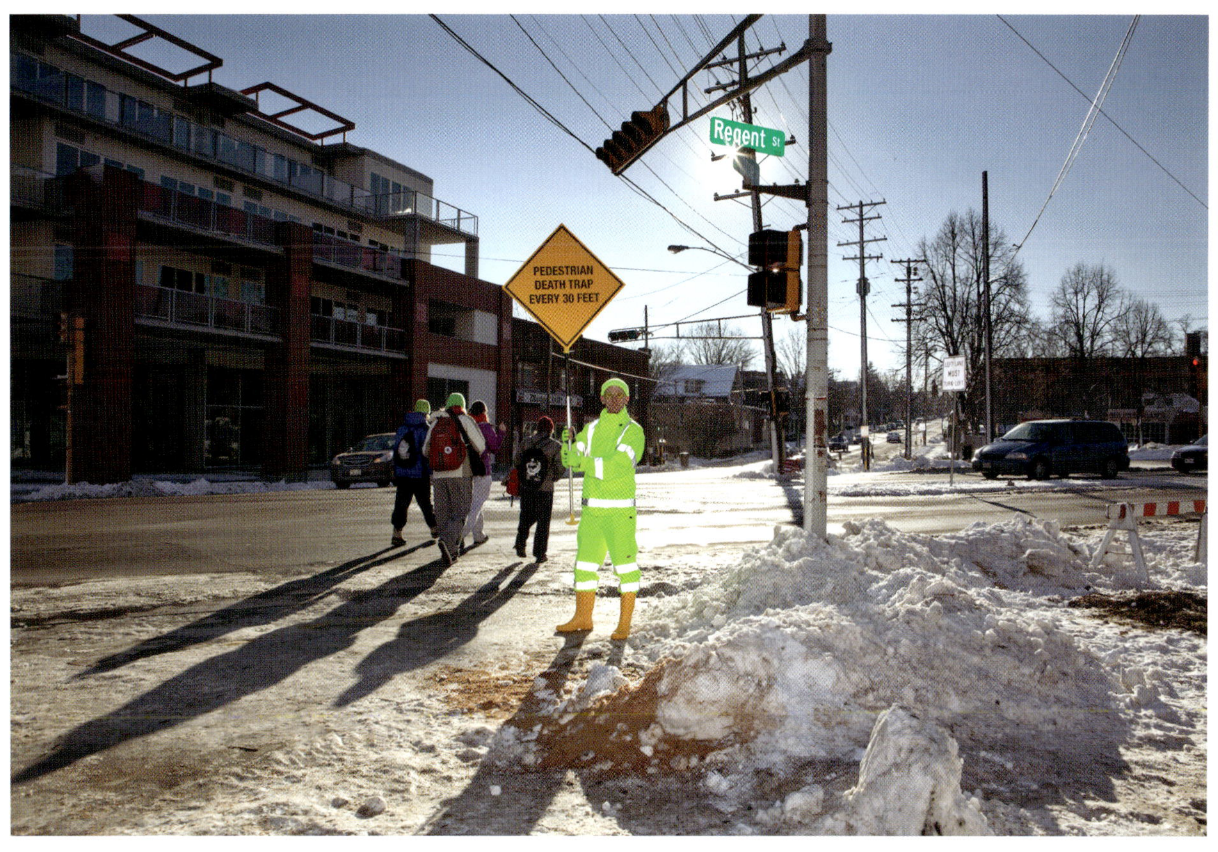

Pedestrian Death Trap, 2011, photograph, 16 x 20 in. (illustrated; not in exhibition)

Recent career achievements

2012 *Structure*, The Rosewood, Abu Dhabi, United Arab Emirates

2011 Visiting Assistant Professor, Foundation for International Education, London, U.K.

2011 *Notting Trunk Hill*, Retail Exodus Reclaim, London, U.K.

2010 *Abstractions and Reflections*, United States Embassy, Addis Ababa, Ethiopia

2008 *National Monotype Exhibition*, Attleboro Arts Museum, Attleboro, Mass.

2008 *Create Chaos*, Orlando Convention Center, Orlando, Fla.

Works in exhibition

Death of an Icon, 2012, mixed media, 70 x 30 x 16 in.

Fragmented Obituary, 2012, mixed media, 70 x 30 x 16 in.

Crosswalk quilt, 2012, mixed media, 70 x 30 x 16 in.

tom
jones

Assistant Professor
UW–Madison Department of Art, since 2006
Photography

2002 Master of Fine Arts, Columbia College, Chicago, Ill.

2002 Master of Arts, Columbia College, Chicago, Ill.

1988 Bachelor of Fine Arts, UW–Madison

"As a member of the Ho-Chunk Nation, Jones is working to photograph his own people in their own communities, in opposition to the many photographs of American Indian people taken by outsiders. He joins a growing group of Native photographers who are expanding the portrayals of Native people with insider perspectives.

"His images from the Ho-Chunk Memorial Day Powwow, held each year in Black River Falls, Wisconsin, celebrate the connections between Ho-Chunk warriors, past and present, and their homes, families and communities. Warriors are an integral part of Ho-Chunk society, honored for their participation in battle and for the wisdom they gained from that experience, and looked up to as leaders and guardians of the people.

"The flagpoles are empty until the morning of Memorial Day, when they receive the service flags of Ho-Chunk veterans. These are the flags presented by the US Armed Forces to the families of deceased veterans. Families fly their veterans' service flags in tribute and in memory on Memorial Day morning as a traditional drum plays and sings a Ho-Chunk flag song. They also serve as mounts for photographs of the veterans, integrating the warriors' images into the powwow just as living warriors are a part of the community. These are not empty, lifeless memorials, but vibrant portraits of individuals and their families at a celebration."—Susan Applegate Krouse, from "A Warrior Celebration: The Photographs of Tom Jones," *Visual Anthropology 19*, no. 3–4 (2006): 295–314.

"

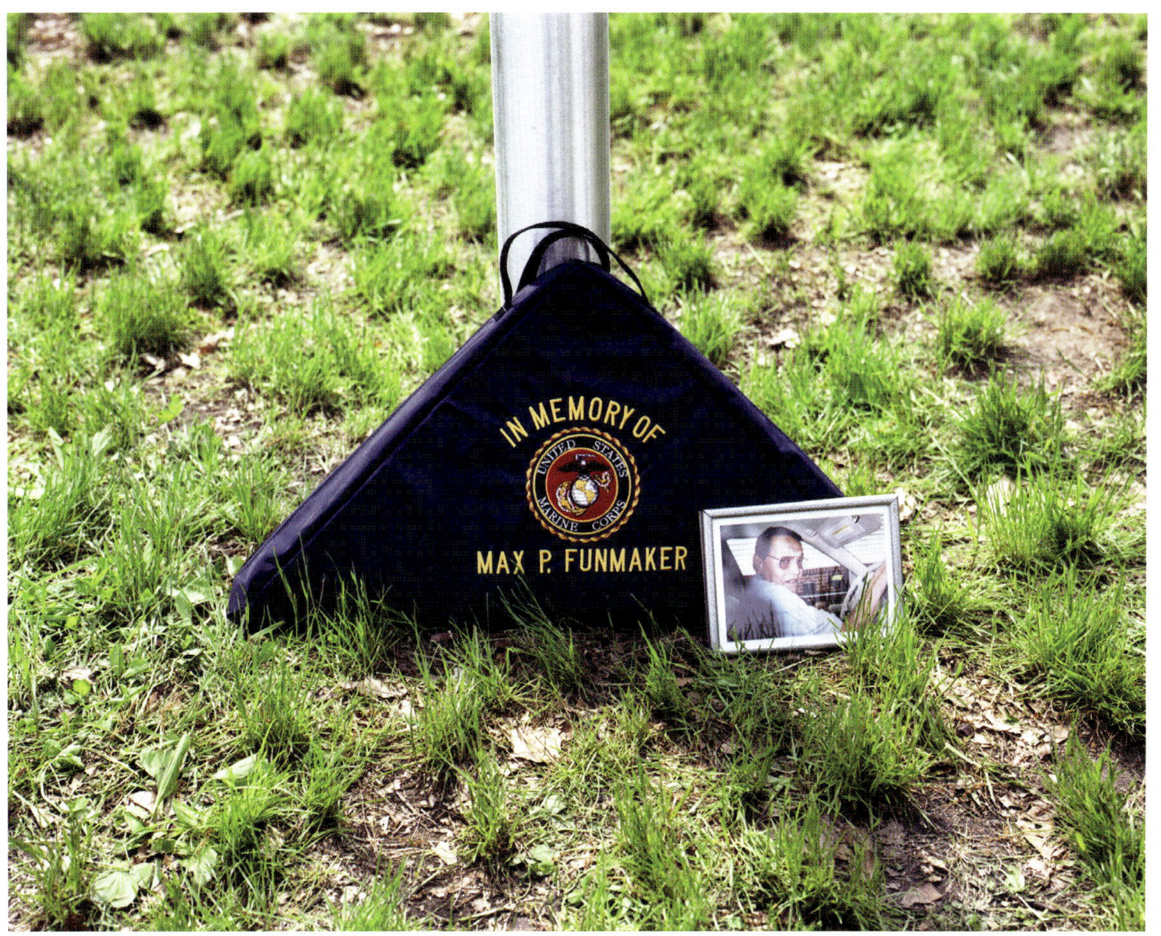

Recent career achievements

2012 Oppenheimer Collection, Nerman Museum of
Contemporary Art, Overland, Kans.

2012 Changing Hands, Museum of Art and Design, New
York, N.Y.

2012 *I am an Indian first and Artist second*, Sherry Leedy
Contemporary Art, Kansas City, Mo.

2011 *People of the Big Voice Photographs of Ho-Chunk
Families by Charles Van Schaick, 1879–1942*, co-author,
Wisconsin Historical Society Press

2011 *Manifestations: New Native American Art Criticism*,
Museum of Contemporary Native Arts

2010 *Mick Gidley, Photography and the USA*, Reaktion
Books, London

2009 *Rendezvoused*, La Biennale di Venezia 53rd international arts exhibition in collaboration with the University of Venice's Department of Postcolonial Literature,
Venice, Italy

Works in exhibition

Max Funmaker, 2011, digital print, 32 x 40 in. (illustrated)

tom
loeser

Professor
UW–Madison Department of Art, since 1991
Wood/Furniture

1993 Master of Fine Arts, University of
Massachusetts

1982 Bachelor of Fine Arts, Boston University

1979 Bachelor of Arts, Haverford College

The work in the exhibition represents three distinct research directions sharing the interest in working in a sketch-like manner, searching for a way to "draw" three-dimensionally with materials that are usually manipulated in a more formal and methodical manner.

The *Fractal Chairs* are miniatures of various scales cut subtractively from a single block of wood, using a band saw and rotating the block in space to remove the negative space and "leave behind" the chairs as a single piece in the end. It's a game of concentration to keep track of what can be cut away without destroying the chairs' structure. A small chair form becomes a structural element, supporting a larger chair form. I'm interested in the multiple scales that exist simultaneously in each structure. The hollow forms of the *Bandsaw Boxes* are puzzles fabricated with both subtractive and additive techniques. The *Roll-Ups* explore seating fabricated as 3-dimensional "sketches" that take advantage of felt's soft and foldable qualities and the brilliant structural capabilities of steel strapping technology developed for the packing and shipping industry.

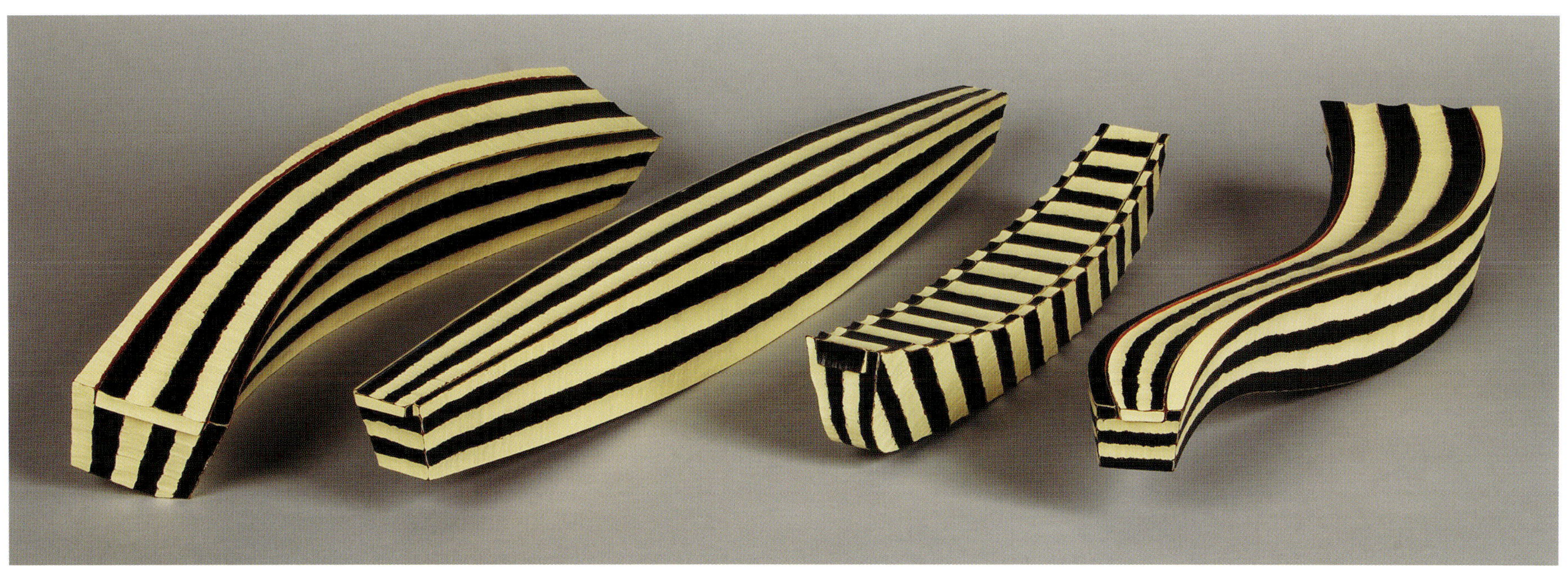

Recent career achievements

2012 *Remixing and Riffing: Postmodernism in Contemporary Wood*, Museum of Art And Design, New York, N.Y.

2011 *Artful Chairs*, Ohio Craft Museum, Columbus, Ohio

2009 *Bridge 10*, Society for Contemporary Craft solo exhibition, Pittsburgh, Penn.

2009 *Boxes and Their Makers*, Messler Gallery, Center for Furniture Craftsmanship, Rockport, Maine

2008 *Flotilla*, Mobilia Gallery solo exhibition, Cambridge, Mass.

Works in exhibition

List, wood, paint, 6 x 31 x 6 in. (illustrated far left)

Tapir, wood, paint, 5 x 37 x 5 in. (center left)

Bob, wood, paint, 5 x 23 x 4 in. (center right)

Sway, wood, paint, 6 x 29 x 6 in. (far right)

Cyrano and Roxanne, 2009, wood, paint, 10 x 29 x 6 in.

Fractal Chairs, 2009–12, wood, paint, dimensions variable

Roll-ups, 2011–12, felt, wood, steel

dennis
miller

Associate Professor
UW–Madison Department of Art, since 2005
Graphic Design

1995 Master of Fine Arts, UW–Madison

1981 Master of Arts, Western Michigan
University, Kalamazoo

1978 Bachelor of Arts, Western Michigan
University, Kalamazoo

Occasionally, people ask me why I'm a graphic designer. My somewhat ungrammatical stock answer is usually something like, "Because it's what I want to do, and I'm good at it." I've also been known to say, "Because other than designing, I'm kind of unemployable." Both answers are true. To put it less glibly, then, I design and teach design because it's interesting, and because it matters. Most of the time, that's enough for me.

More recently, I've also wanted to excite students about becoming serious practitioners who are passionate about the craft. Even better, when a student has an idea that's fresh, funny, true, and/or breaks the rules in a way that makes aesthetic theory and convention seem irrelevant, it's the student who ends up giving the lesson, and the teacher who gets to learn something new.

So … maybe there's a third answer to the question. I'm still a graphic designer, after all these years and a roller coaster career, because it's fun.

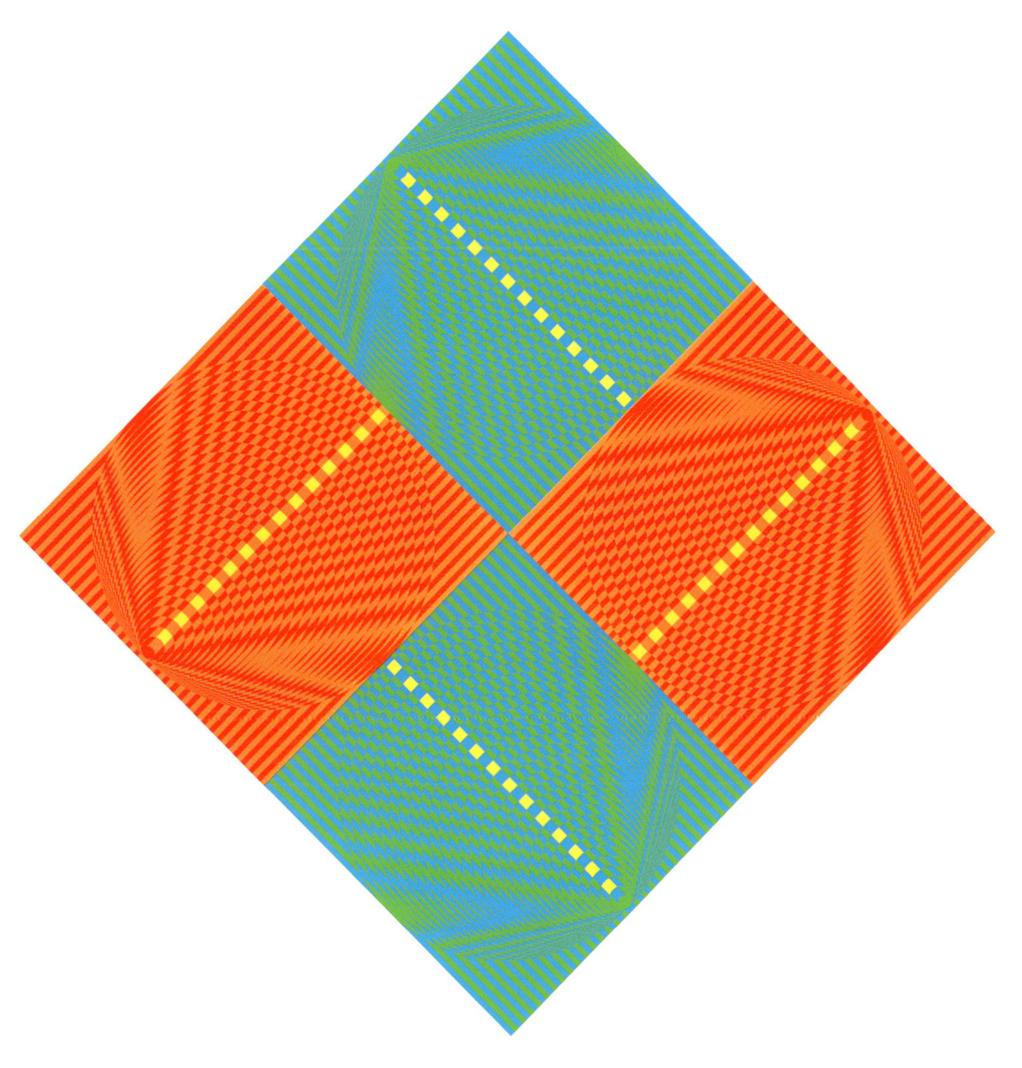

Recent career achievements

2011 *Graphic Intervention: 26 years of International AIDS Awareness Posters*, Art Directors Club, New York, N.Y.

2010 *Uncanny: Surrealism and Graphic Design, 24th International Biennial of Graphic Design*, Moravian Gallery, Brno, Czech Republic

2009 *International Poster and Graphic Arts Exhibition*, Chaumont, France

2008 *Golden Bee 8: Moscow International Biennale of Graphic Design*, Moscow, Russian Federation

Works in exhibition

Pattern Study 1, 2011, Adobe Illustrator 5.5 and Fontographer 5, inkjet print, 24 x 24 in. (illustrated)

Pattern Study 2, 2011, Adobe Illustrator 5.5 and Fontographer 5, inkjet print, 24 x 24 in.

Pattern Study 3, 2011, Adobe Illustrator 5.5 and Fontographer 5, inkjet print, 24 x 24 in.

Pattern Study 4, 2011, Adobe Illustrator 5.5 and Fontographer 5, inkjet print, 24 x 24 in.

Pattern Study 5, 2011, Adobe Illustrator 5.5 and Fontographer 5, inkjet print, 24 x 24 in.

Pattern Study 6, 2011, Adobe Illustrator 5.5 and Fontographer 5, inkjet print, 24 x 24 in.

meg
mitchell

Assistant Professor
UW–Madison Department of Art, since 2011
Digital Foundations

2008 Master of Fine Arts, University
of Maryland

2004 Bachelor of Fine Arts, University
of South Florida

My practice traverses the boundaries of the conceptual/linguistic world and the physical world. I have a long-standing attraction to the material imperfections that emerge from a collision of these two modes of experiencing reality. My use of ephemeral materials in tandem with rigid systems exaggerates this contrast, suggesting the divide between a linguistic, conceptual space and an inherently organic and unpredictable physical space.

The piece in this exhibition re-creates Umberto Eco's seminal essay on semiotics "Signs and the Role of the Reader" as a physical object that can be pulled and reshaped by the viewer in physical space.

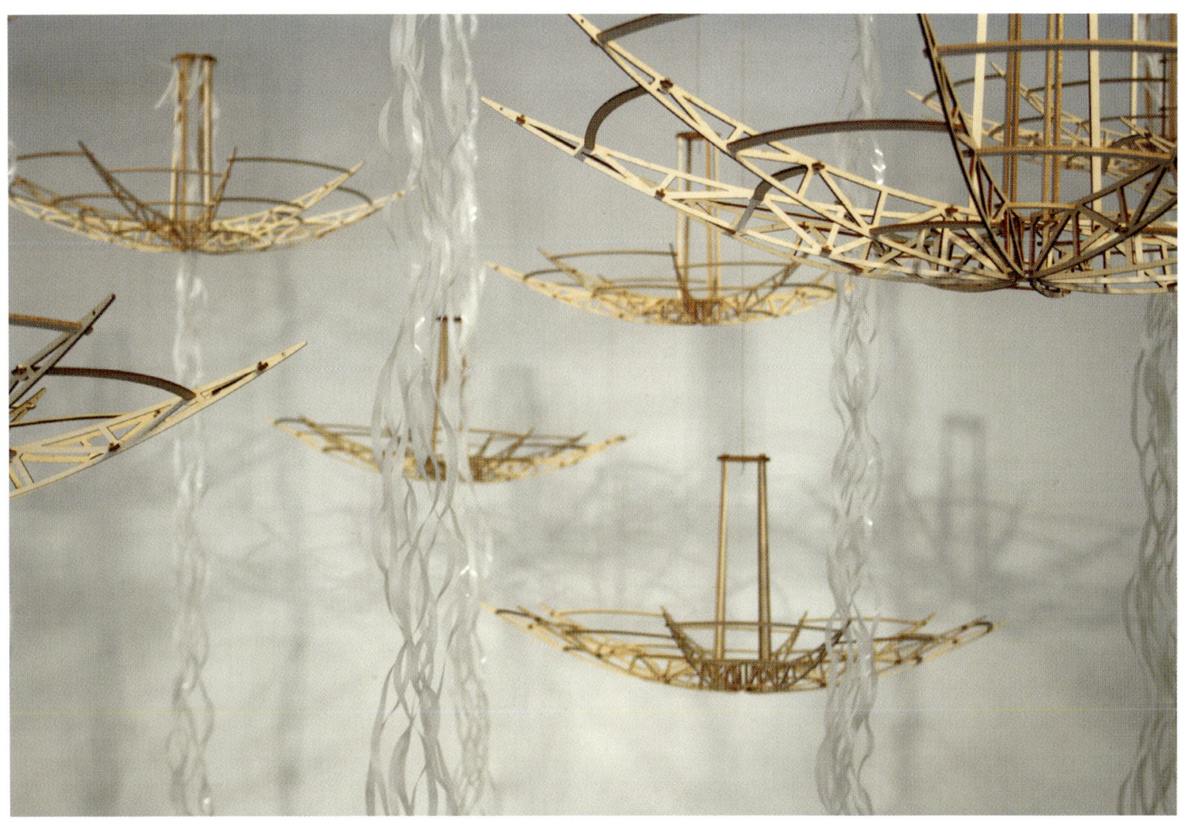

Recent career achievements

2011 *Visualizing Difference (birds of a feather)*, Hartnett
Gallery solo exhibition, Rochester, N.Y.

2010 Representing Difference through Embodied Data,
4th Annual Upgrade! International Conference, Sao
Paulo, Brazil

2010 *Meg Mitchell*, Harris House Gallery solo exhibition,
Atlantic Center for the Arts, New Symrna Beach, Fla.

2010 *Wild Culture: Ecological Perspectives*, Roy C. Moore
Art Gallery solo exhibition, Gainesville State College,
Gainesville, Ga.

2008 Profiled by J.W. Mahoney, "Report from Washington
D.C.: To a Different Drum," *Art in America*, May 2008

2007 Jessica Dawson, "They've Made a Mockery of the
Color School," *The Washington Post*

Works in exhibition

signs (and the role of the reader), 2011, mixed media,
approx. 12 x 12 x 12 ft. installed (detailed illustrated)

nancy
mladenoff

Professor
UW–Madison Department of Art, since 1999
Painting and Drawing

1987 Master of Fine Arts, School of the
Art Institute of Chicago

1982 Bachelor of Science, UW–Madison

My studio practice over the past several years has concentrated on mixed-media oil painting, flashe/gouache, and watercolor delving into ideas of natural history, botany, entomology, ornithology, geography, and history as they relate to contemporary culture. My current research involves the work of early American women naturalists, earth and animal scientists, explorers, outlaws, musicians and athletes who lived during the 18th through 20th centuries. My paintings are a metaphorical classification of female mentors/alter egos that is grounded in the past but can be relevant to present concerns in contemporary painting. Notions of the anti-heroic in much of contemporary painting have very little relevance for women as we have limited or no history of the heroic in our past. Through the work, I seek to learn about the history and lives of American women who were driven to make significant accomplishments beyond wife and mother, against a considerably unsupportive culture. The imagery that is created reflects my conceptual, philosophical, and psychological interests that engage with issues in contemporary art.

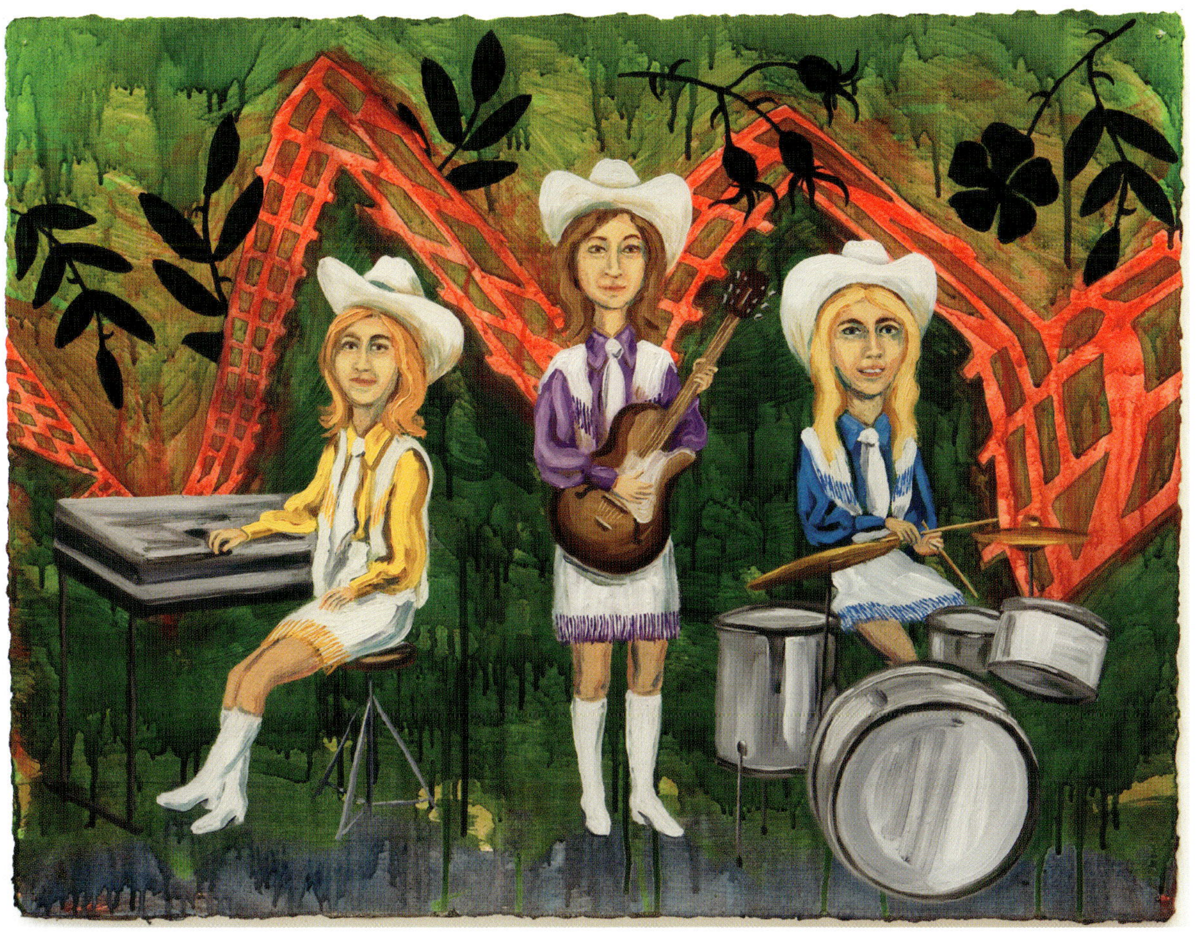

Recent career achievements

2011 *Biome Series*, McKinley Arts & Culture Center solo exhibition, Gallery East, Reno, Nev.

2010 *German Plants, Birds & Insects*, International Forest Art Center (IWZ) solo exhibition, Darmstadt, Germany

2009 *Post-Audubon: Birds & Insects*, The Arsenal Gallery solo exhibition, New York, N.Y.

2006 *Between the Lakes*, Madison Museum of Contemporary Art group exhibition, Madison, Wisc.

2005 *Carry On*, Feigen Contemporary group exhibition, New York, N.Y.

2005 *New Photographs*, Cultural Exchange Station solo exhibition, Tabor, Czech Republic

2005 *New Photographs*, Lademoen Kunstnerverksteder solo exhibition, Trondheim, Norway

Works in exhibition

The Ladies, 2011, series of oil on paper and flashe on paper, 16 x 20 in. to 23 x 30 in. each (illustrated)

frances
myers

Professor
UW–Madison Department of Art, since 1988
Printmaking, Digital Media, Video

1965 Master of Fine Arts, UW–Madison

1963 Master of Science, UW–Madison

1962 Bachelor of Science, UW–Madison

I think of my photos/prints of the interior of the original 1917 Sterling Hall—built for the Physics Department at the UW–Madison—as salvage, records documenting the erasure of a relic.

The spaces in these photographs could be considered "site reports," visually informing what remains. From 2008 to 2010 I freely enter Sterling Hall after the Physics Department had moved out. The building was being dismantled, day by day, month by month, stripped of its contents except for skeletons of lab paraphernalia and debris casually tossed to the floor. One day I would slip into an office where shelves full of ancient notations were stored, only to find the contents disappeared the next time I came. I felt an almost mystical connection to the building and what, for a brief time, still remained.

A few of my images replay the event in 1970 when the newer part of Sterling Hall was blown up as a reaction to the experiments by the U.S. Army Math Center that would extend our presence in Vietnam. The explosion caused the death of a researcher and the destruction of four floors of the building—but not the Math Center.

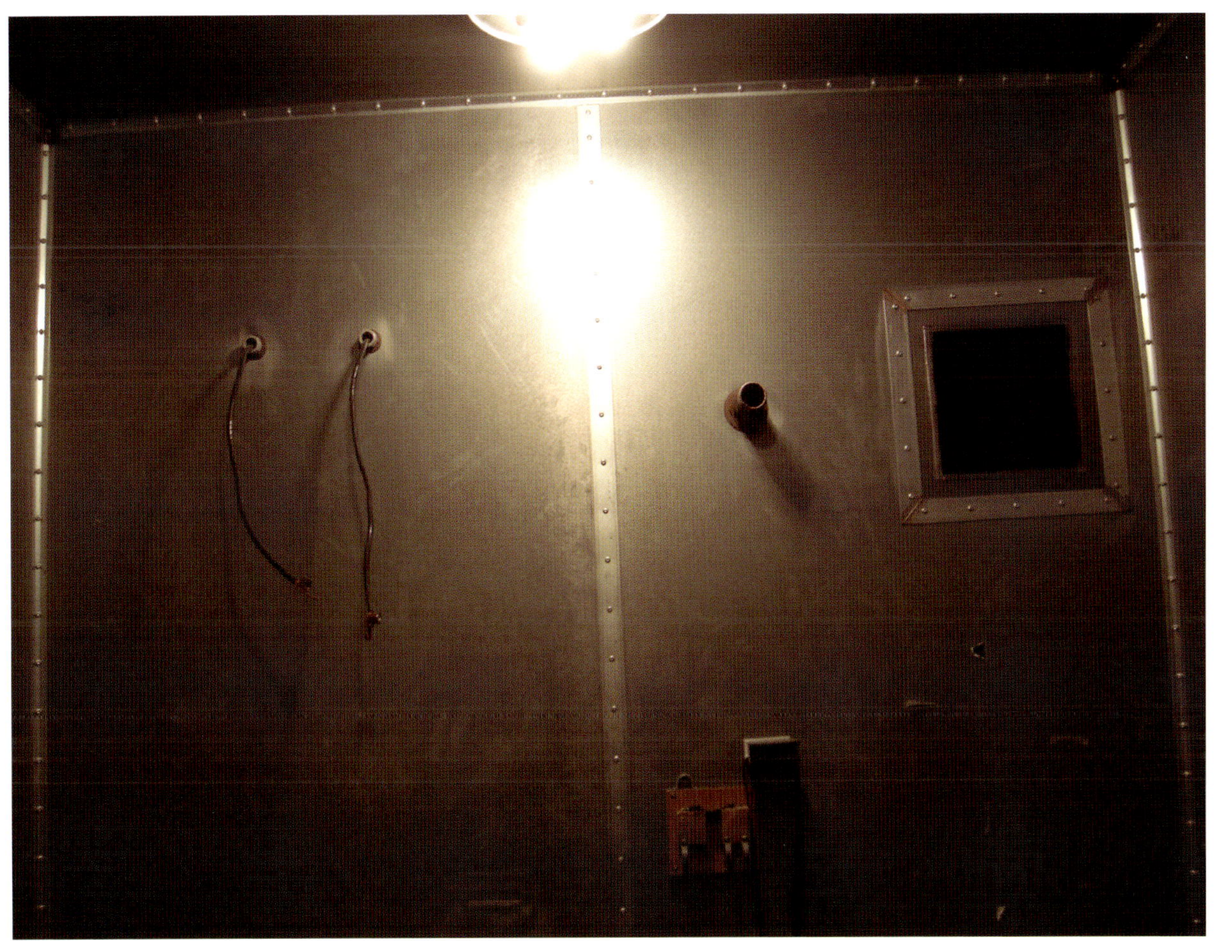

Recent career achievements

2011 *Post-Mortem*, Perimeter Gallery solo exhibition, Chicago, Ill.

2011 *FLWright Portfolio*, Racine Art Museum solo exhibition, Racine, Wisc.

2011 *Site Reports*, Grace Chosy Gallery two-person exhibition, Madison, Wisc.

2011 *Southern Graphics Council International Traveling Print Exhibition* juror

2010 *Wisconsin Triennial of Contemporary Art*, Madison Museum of Contemporary Art group exhibition and catalogue, Madison, Wisc.

2009 *184th Annual Exhibition of Contemporary American Art*, National Academy Museum group exhibition and catalogue, New York, N.Y.

Works in exhibition

Post-Mortem, 2009–11, archival digital prints, seven-part installation, 14 1/2 x 7 ft. (part 4 illustrated)

Explosion Inside, 2011, archival digital print, 39 1/2 x 76 in.

leslee
nelson

Professor
UW–Madison Department of Art, since 1984
Embroidery, Vintage Textiles

1978 Master of Fine Arts, UW–Madison

1977 Master of Science, UW–Madison

1972 Bachelor of Fine Arts, California
College of the Arts

Inspired by *Voices of Women (Amazwi Abesifazane)*, embroidered memories from South African Apartheid, I began using my mother's and grandmother's linen napkins, tablecloths, and tea towels as a way to tell my own stories. I first stitched my childhood misperceptions, stories of love, and travel adventures. Later works focused on the way my parents' favoritism for my brother led to moments of confrontation and then reconnection. This meditative process allowed me to accept and forgive. When my mother was hospitalized last year, I again turned to embroidering to work through thoughts, feelings, and memories, a process that continued up to and after her death.

When I began, I wondered whether it was appropriate to use a technique that recorded the horrific violence of Apartheid to tell stories from my protected Midwestern, middle-class, middle-child's life. Stories that inspired me centered on the power of deep discovery, forgiveness, and healing. My own embroidered reflections on pain, recovery, misunderstanding, love, and laughter celebrate the creative spirit of the women who opened my path.

The piece illustrated here is based on a quote from *The Transition Handbook: From Oil Dependency to Local Resilience.*

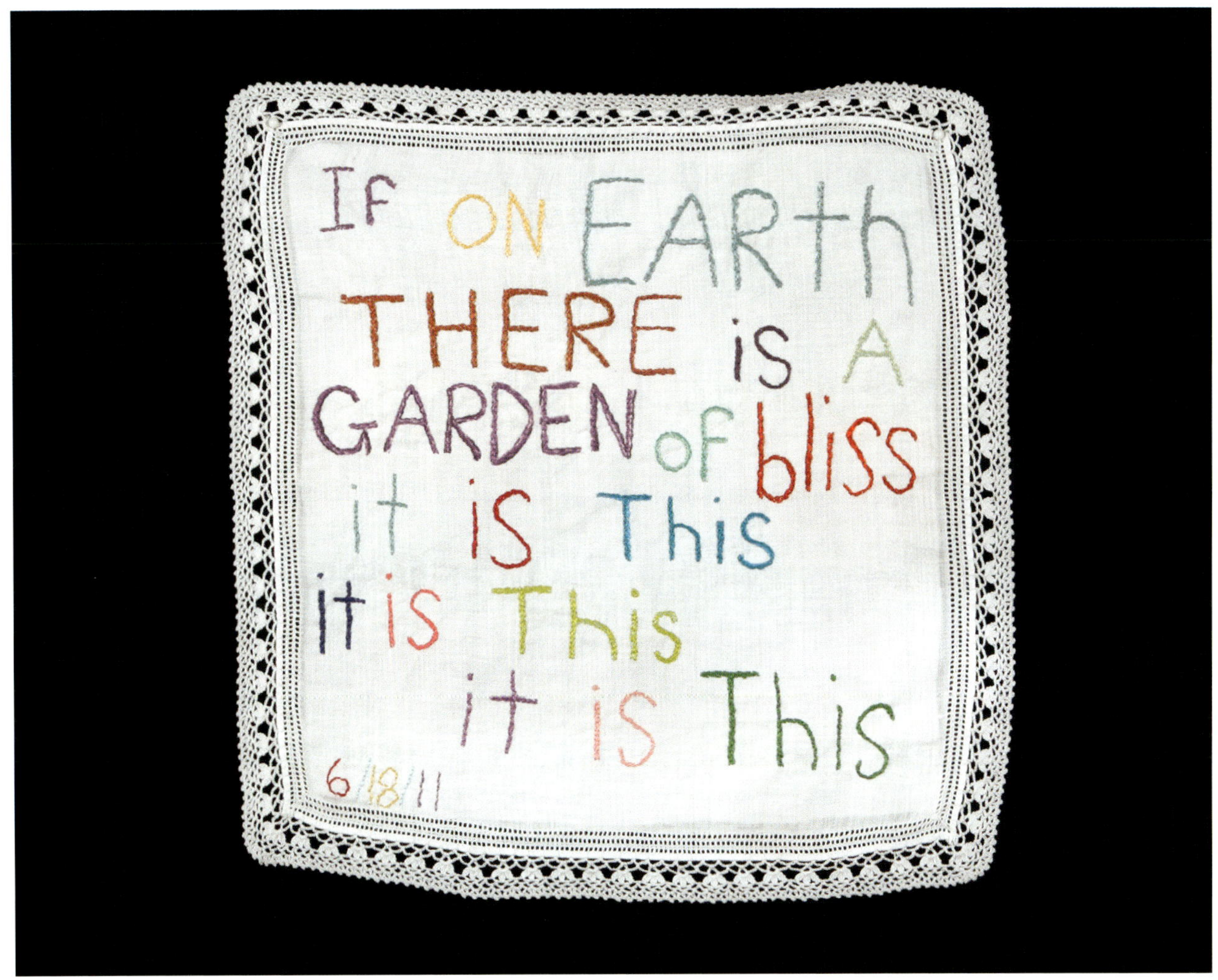

Recent career achievements

2011 Rockford College Art Gallery solo exhibition,
Rockford, Ill.

2010 *Story Time*, Islip Art Museum, Islip, N.Y.

2009 Mariposa Gallery solo exhibition,
Albuquerque, N.M.

2009 Galerìa Tonantzin solo exhibition,
San Antonio, Tex.

2008 Published in *Memory Cloths*, Blessings Press,
Madison, Wisc.

2008 Public Collections, Nek Chand
Museum, Chandigarh, India

Works in exhibition

Memory Cloths, 2008–11, embroidered found fabrics,
variable sizes for a total of 6 x 10 ft.
Garden of Bliss, 2011, silk embroidery, linen handkerchief,
11 1/2 x 11 1/2 in. (illustrated)

douglas
rosenberg

Professor

UW–Madison Department of Art, since 2006
Video, Performance, Installation

1985 Master of Fine Arts, San Francisco Art Institute

For many years, my work has been formally situated at the intersection of performance and the moving image. Most recently, this work manifests as projects in which art, life, and community merge into a seamless practice. I have attempted to create spaces for contemplation that are seasonal, geographically specific, and attuned to ritual and the allure of the local.

These projects include video installations meant to record my own focused engagement with the landscape and my surroundings and to also act as free-standing meditations.

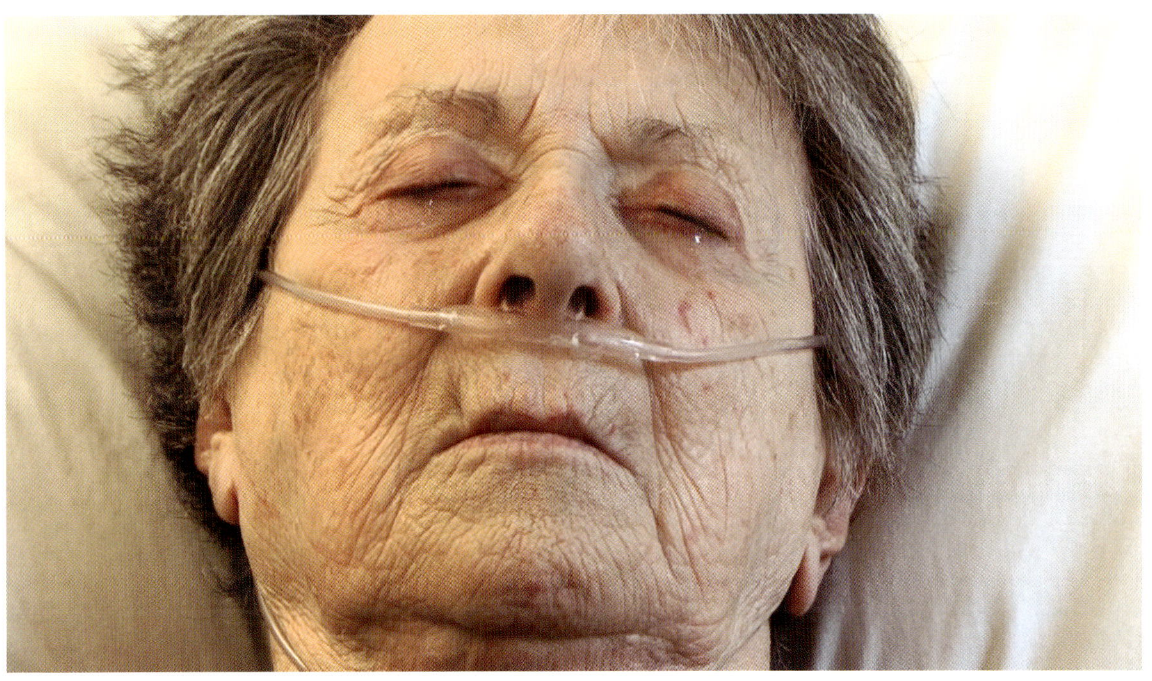

Recent career achievements

2010 *Douglas Rosenberg, Retrospective*, Agite y Serva Festival of Video Dance, Puebla, Mexico

2010 *Wisconsin Triennial Exhibition*, Madison Museum of Contemporary Art, Madison, Wisc.

2009 Short-listed for Barcelona Prize, Festival of Dance and the Moving Image, Barcelona, Spain, Caixa

2009 Mostra Internacional de Vídeo-Dança, Dance Without Shadow, São Luiz Teatro Municipal, Lisbon, Portugal

2009 *Douglas Rosenberg, Retrospective*, International Festival De VideoDanza, Centro Cultural de Ricoletta, Buenos Aires, Argentina

2003 EMMY Nomination for Outstanding Achievement for Single Entertainment Program or Series

Works in exhibition

Stills from *Meditation (Mother)* 2012, video installation (illustrated)

paul
sacaridiz

Associate professor
UW–Madison Department of Art, since 2007
Ceramics

1998 Master of Fine Arts, School of the Art
Institute of Chicago

1993 Bachelor of Fine Arts, New York State
College of Ceramics at Alfred University

My work is a response to considering systems of abstraction and the seemingly impossible task of understanding something in its entirety. Past projects have looked at the visual correlation between domestic objects, such as decorative food molds, and the actual structures of built architecture. Presented on custom-built platforms, the works refer to architect's trestle-style drafting tables with arrangements of objects carefully situated on elevated risers. The work is highly constructed, with a certain sculptural logic that is both pragmatic and allusive at the same time.

An incomplete articulation, included in this exhibition, utilizes the conceptual framework of a schematic diagram to point toward differing ways of articulating form. Sagging mounds of ceramic extrusions are situated alongside precise mathematical models and awkward structural forms. Individual components are physically and conceptually networked together, creating an elaborate three-dimensional system of mapping that becomes suggestive of propositional models and utopian systems.

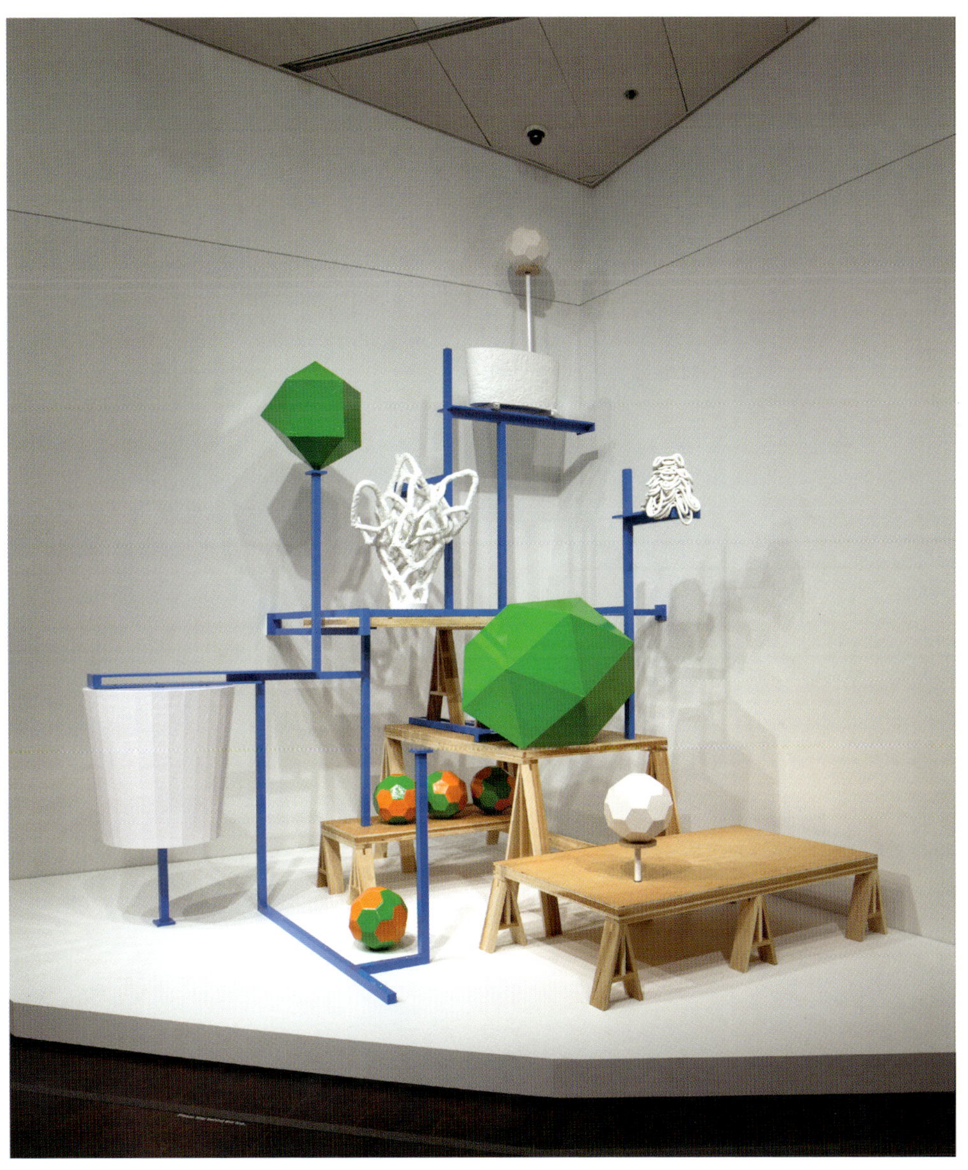

Recent career achievements

2011 *Overthrown*, Denver Art Museum, Denver, Colo.

2011 Nominee: The Louis Comfort Tiffany Foundation Artist Grant

2011 Panelist: *Overthrown: The State of Contemporary Ceramics*, DAM contemporaries, Denver Art Museum, Denver, Colo.

2010 *Interactions in Clay: Contemporary Explorations of the Collection*, Philadelphia Museum of Art, Philadelphia, Penn.

2010 *Wisconsin Triennial*, Madison Museum of Contemporary Art. Madison, Wisc.

Select residencies: Art/Industry Program at Kohler Company, the Ragdale Foundation, the Vermont Studio Center, the Watershed Center for the Ceramic Arts

Works in exhibition

an incomplete articulation, 2011, ceramic, wood, powder-coated aluminium, cut vinyl, board, 12 x 12 x 15 ft. (Photo courtesy of the Denver Art Muesum)

elaine
scheer

Professor
UW–Madison Department of Art, since 1990
Mixed Media

1982 Master of Fine Arts, San Francisco
Art Institute

1979 Bachelor of Fine Arts, Sonoma State
University

I dream I am flying over my neighborhood. I can see houses, trees, and the railroad tracks behind my house. I look inside my house as if I were a small bird who flew in. Of course everything is neat and tidy. After making a painting of my neighborhood I looked up my street on Google Earth; I could only see trees, no houses; the railroad tracks are straight.

I have been making bird's-eye-view paintings of the Madison area from memory, maps, and the internet. I love the immediacy of watercolor on paper. Turning big swaths of color into brush-stroke patterns, I am inspired by the many tiny stitches and silk threads my mother uses in her embroidery.

I enjoy being part of the creative hum of the new Art Lofts studios, with colleagues and students working away. After serving as department chair, I love the intimacy of teaching watercolor. I am continually challenged by our students who are so hard working, smart, and creative.

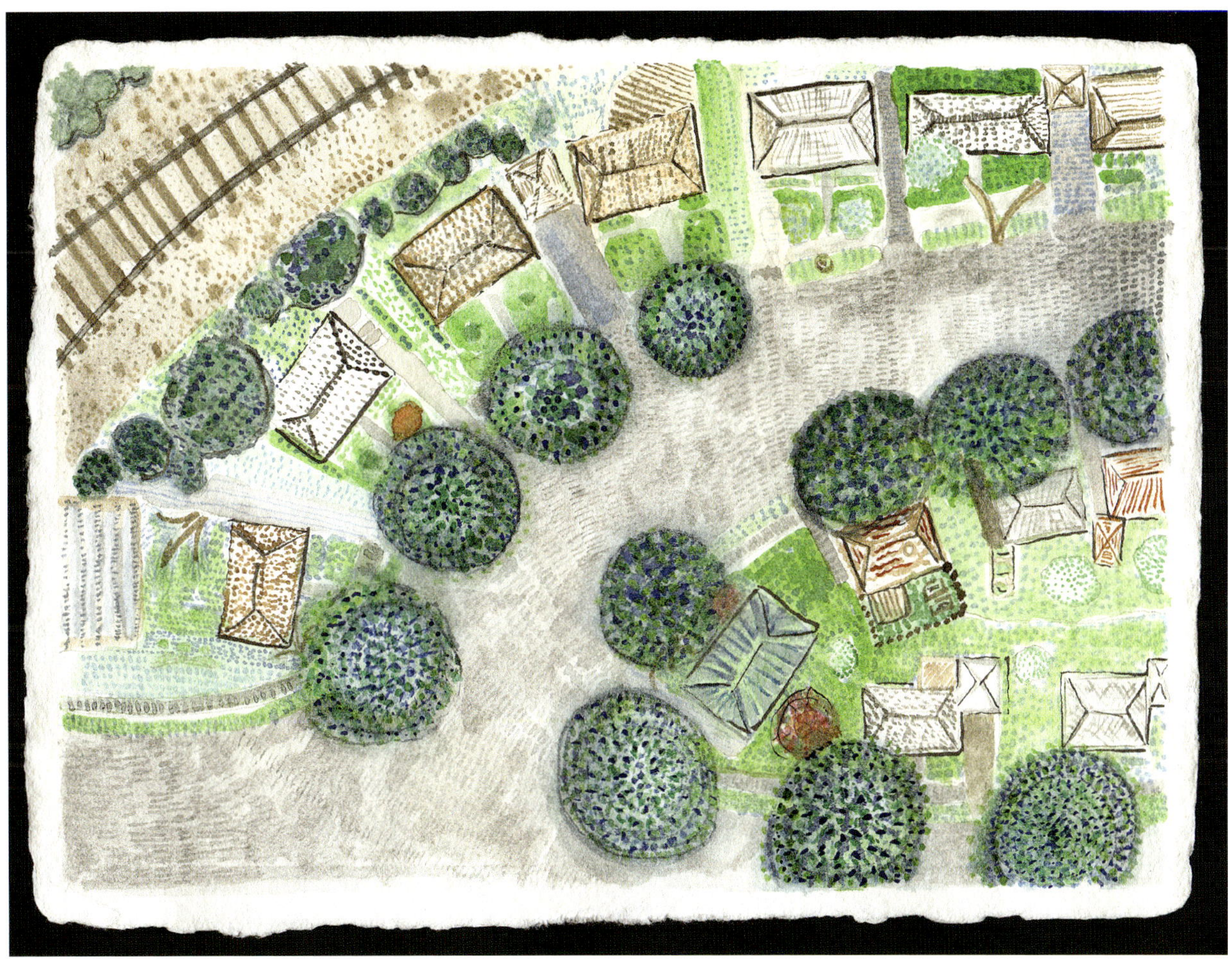

Recent career achievements

When I was a student, I lived for spending time in the studio, and exhibits and notoriety meant a great deal to me. Having been included in many exhibits, along with the honor of nice awards, I have found that the work is what gives me the most pleasure. When I am painting I feel that I am doing what I should be doing.

Works in exhibition

Lorraine turns into Dahlen, 2011, watercolor, 5 3/4 x 8 in. (illustrated)

gail
simpson

Professor
UW–Madison Department of Art, since 2000
Foundations Coordinator, Sculpture

1988 Master of Fine Arts, School of the Art
Institute of Chicago

1977 Bachelor of Fine Arts, Washington
University

I am a sculptor and public artist who works on projects individually and as part of *Actual Size*, a collaborative team. I am interested in what artist-citizens can contribute to public space and to public life. I usually work in an architecturally integrated manner but enjoy the freedom afforded by temporary projects as well. With this work I had an opportunity to use fallen trees as a result of a series of storms. These hollow logs are lit from within to produce imagery on their "faces." The imagery of the shadows consists of natural phenomena that could be construed as foreboding or prophetic—swarms of birds, meteor showers, eclipses. I hope the sculptures are creating an effect similar to a *nature morte* still life—a meditation on the passage of time and the ephemerality of life.

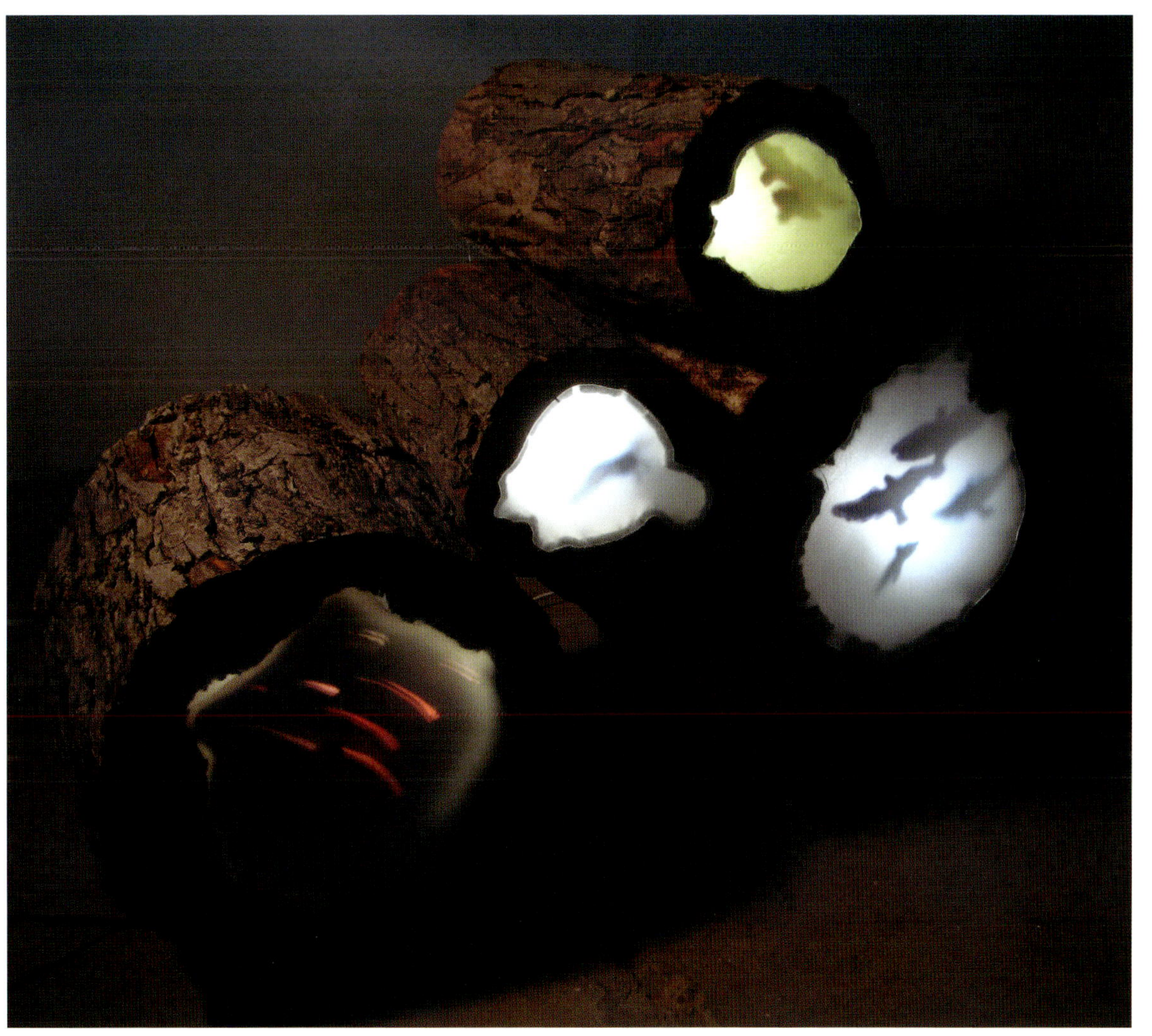

Recent career achievements

2011 Commission for Dwight Foster Public Library, Ft. Atkinson, Wisc.

2011 *The Gift*, in *Nature Unframed* temporary public art project at Morton Arboretum, Lisle, Ill. (as part of *Actual Size*)

2011 *PopUp Art Loop*, Chicago Loop Alliance temporary space solo exhibition

2010 Best in show, *2010 Outdoor Sculpture Exhibit*, Cary, N.C. (as part of *Actual Size*)

2009 Public art commission, Warch Student Center, Lawrence University, Appleton, Wisc. (as part of *Actual Size*)

2009 Commission for Northwest Medical Clinic, Charlotte, N.C.

Works in exhibition

Illuminated Woods, 2011, hollow logs and light, 10 x 8 x 4 ft. (illustrated)

leslie
smith III

Assistant Professor
UW–Madison Department of Art, since 2011
Life Drawing/Painting

2009 Master of Fine Arts, Yale University
School of Art

2007 Bachelor of Fine Arts, Maryland
Institute College of Art

My studio practice is concentrated around visual abstraction as a method for communicating political anguish. I make both small and large narrative abstract paintings in addition to works on papers. Currently, I am focused on psychological trauma as something we violently inflict on each other, as an effect of human power dynamics, resulting in a series of works that portray the nature of fear, anxiety, and post-traumatic stress among other negative aspects of the human experience.

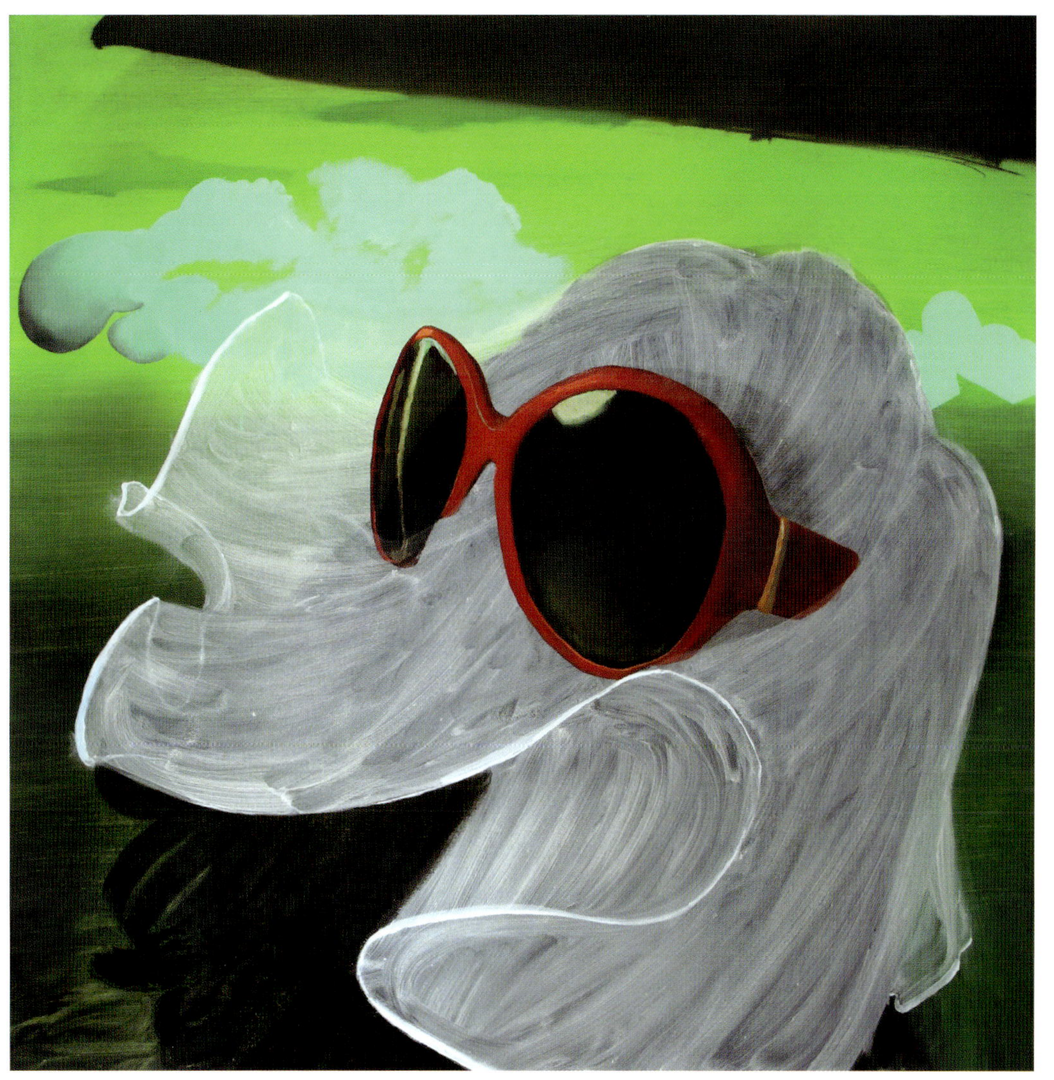

Recent career achievements

2011 *Two Men 2011: Tim Roseborough & Leslie Smith, III,* Strivers Gardens Gallery group exhibition, New York, N.Y.

2010 *Balls,* Obsidian Arts group exhibition, Minneapolis, Minn.

2010 *In/Ex,* Gallery M group exhibition, New York, N.Y.

2010 *Joel Dean, Fabienne Lasserre, Leslie Smith III,* Jolie Laide Gallery group exhibition, Philadelphia, Penn.

2009 American Academy in Rome, Al Held Affiliate Fellow, Rome, Italy

2008 *Verge,* Galapagos Art Space group exhibition, New York, N.Y.

2007 *Visions of Conflict: Rendering Dissent,* Gormley Gallery College of Notre Dame group exhibition, Baltimore, Md.

Works in exhibition

Creeper, oil on canvas, 40 x 58 in.

Room, oil on canvas, 40 x 58 in.

Runaway, 2011, oil on canvas, 48 x 48 in. (illustrated; not in exhibition)

t.l. solien

Professor
UW–Madison Department of Art, since 1997
Painting, Drawing, Printmaking

1977 Master of Fine Arts, University of
Nebraska

1973 Bachelor of Arts, Moorhead State
University, Minn.

I am interested in examining and manipulating the objective and textual artifacts of 19th- and early-20th-century American history. I hope to discover, characterize, re-imagine and re-constitute—*as contemporary artworks*—the many human narratives of accomplishment and failure, joyfulness and tragedy that met these immigrants and indigenous peoples on their journey, and the experiences awaiting them in the American western frontier. I hope to suggest, allegorically, perpetual and timeless aspects of the human experience, both devastating and enabling, as well as the mercurial ethics of governmental, corporate, and societal imperatives.

As has been the case with aspects of my research and studio practice over the last decade of exploring historical themes and events, I am not interested in making traditional history paintings grounded in realism or naturalism, nor am I interested in illustrating a self-contained *historical* moment. I am interested in developing contemporary artworks that challenge and reconstitute the nature of historical referentiality, challenge the conventions of visual narrative structure, and reveal a timeless, repetitive, and inescapable aspect of the human experience.

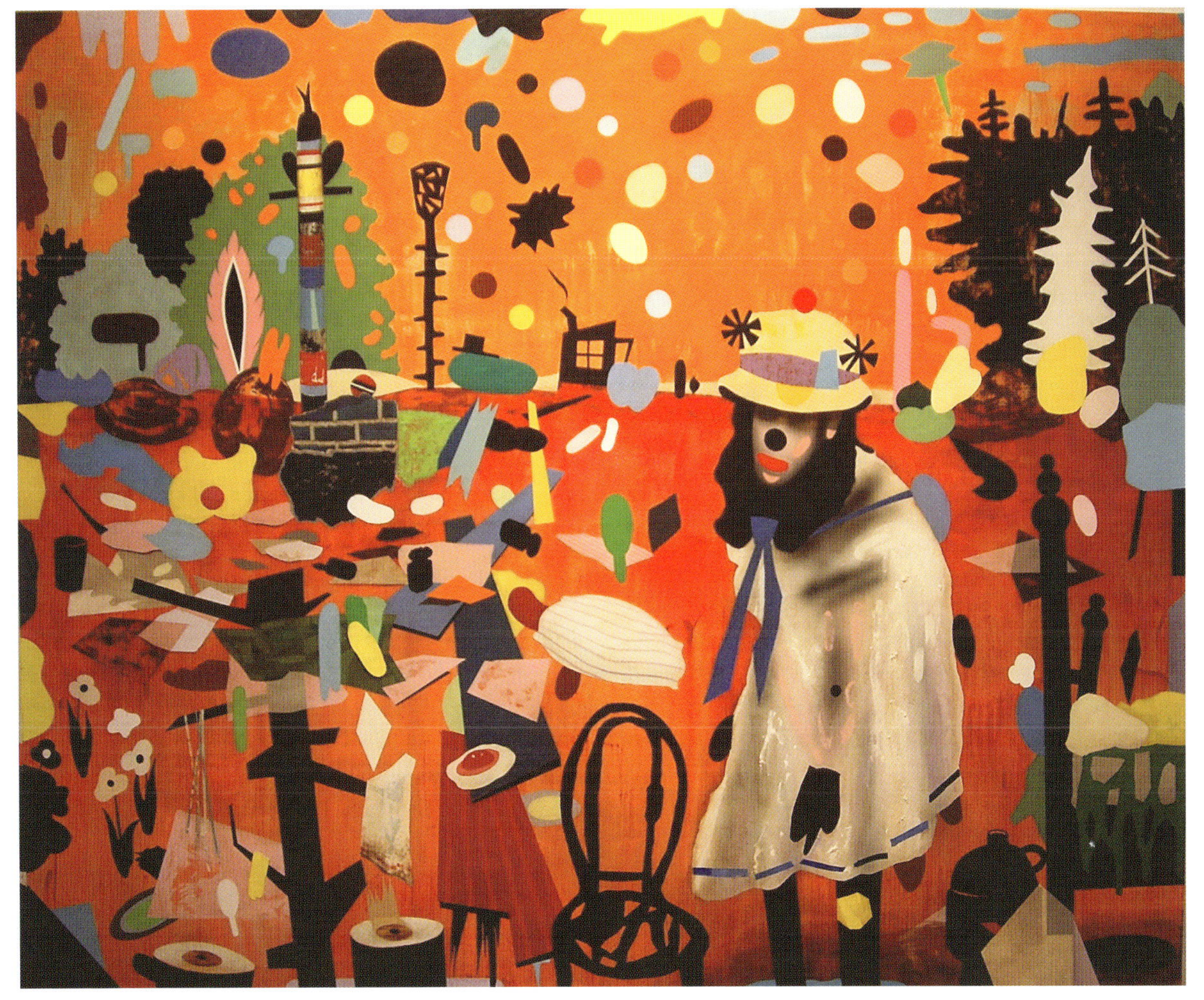

Significant career achievements

2011 Vilas Research Fellowship, UW–Madison

2010 Wisconsin State Arts Board Individual Artist Grant

2008 Joan Mitchell Foundation Fellowship in Painting

2008 *TL Solien: Myths and Monsters*, Madison Museum of Contemporary Art, Madison, Wisc.

1987 *Avant-Garde in the Eighties*, Los Angeles County Museum of Art group exhibition, Calif.

1985 *39th Biennial of American Painting*, Corcoran Museum group exhibition, Washington, D.C.

1983 *Whitney Biennial 1983*, Whitney Museum of American Art group exhibition, New York, N.Y.

Works in exhibition

Wasteland, 2009–10, acrylic and oil on canvas, 78 x 96 in. (illustrated)

fred
stonehouse

Assistant Professor
UW–Madison Department of Art, since 2008
Life Drawing, Painting

1982 Bachelor of Fine Arts, UW–Milwaukee

Downtown Milwaukee in the mid-1960s was an adult world of hotels, office buildings, and fine department stores. On a summer afternoon in 1966, I walked holding my father's hand, window-shopping along the way. We passed the USO, sailors lounging out front smoking cigarettes. I had no idea what our destination was, and when we stopped at the final window my jaw dropped. My interest in tattooing and tattoo art has been an important part of my visual vocabulary since that first vivid experience of imagery lining the walls of Amund Dietzel's Milwaukee tattoo parlor.

Hand-painted tattoo designs are known as "flash," a term that dates to the days when tattoo booths were common on the carnival midway. The images were designed for maximum graphic impact and they appealed to one's sense of romance, adventure, daring, or sentimentality. Pierced hearts, skulls, daggers, panthers, and flowers are as popular today as they were 100 years ago.

My project is both homage to the historical tradition of tattooing and a piece of historical fiction. The booth is not historically accurate, but will manifest a filtered and slightly skewed recollection of tattoo shops from my childhood. The flash will be slightly wrong, the scale of the booth too small to actually function, and the exterior correct in spirit but completely imagined in its details.

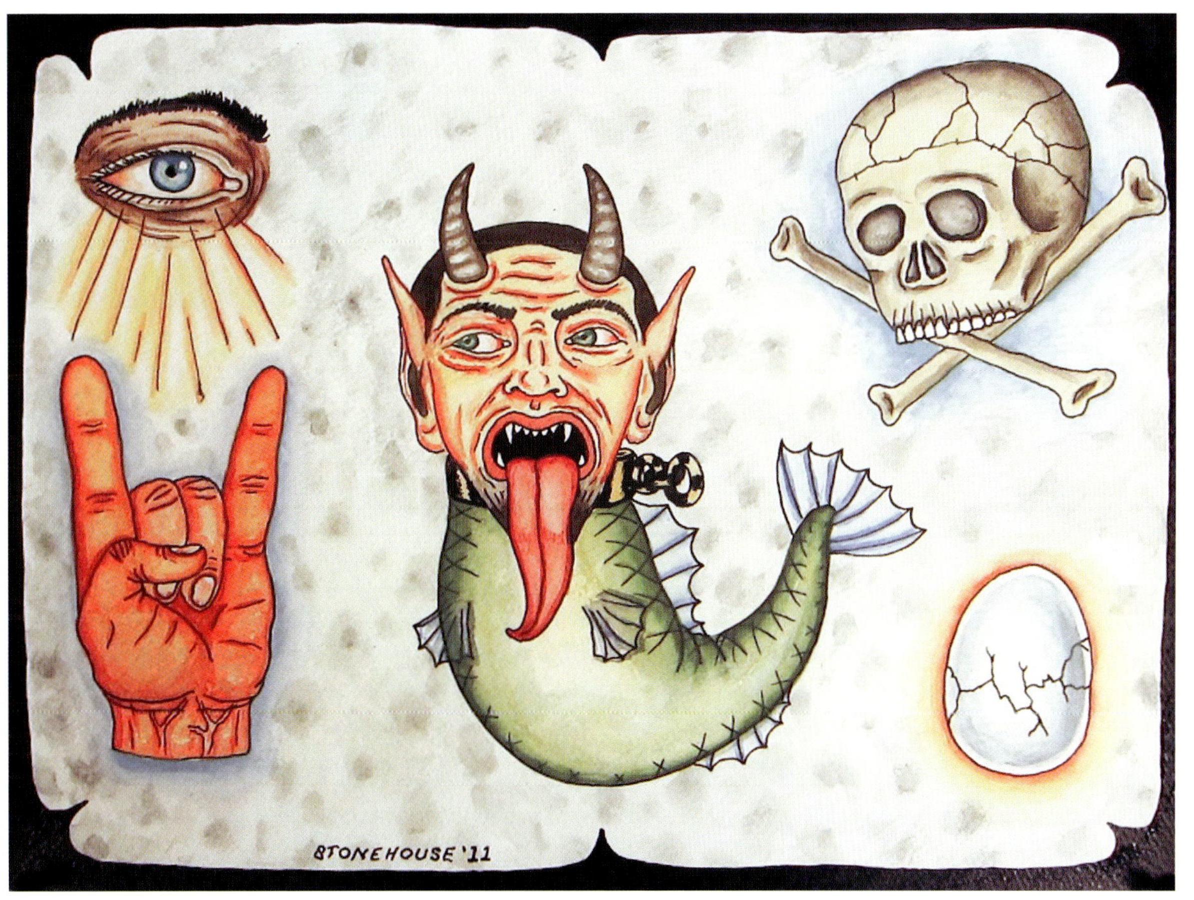

Recent career achievements

2011 *Fred Stonehouse, The Deacon's Seat*, Sarah Moody Gallery solo exhibition, University of Alabama, Tuscaloosa, Ala.

2011 *Marsh Night*, Koplin Del Rio Gallery solo exhibition, Los Angeles, Calif.

2010 *Marshland*, Howard Scott Gallery solo exhibition, New York, N.Y.

2010 *Alchemy and Image*, Rockford Art Museum group exhibition, Rockford, Ill.

2010 *Neo Fabulists*, Feinkunst Kruger group exhibition, Hamburg, Germany

2007 *Fred Stonehouse, Painting*, Tammen Galerie solo exhibition, Berlin, Germany

Works in exhibition

Tattoo Flash #1, 2011, watercolor, 11 x 15 in. (illustrated)

Stoney's Tiny Tattoo, 2011, painted wood construction with framed watercolor paintings, 96 x 48 x 48 in.

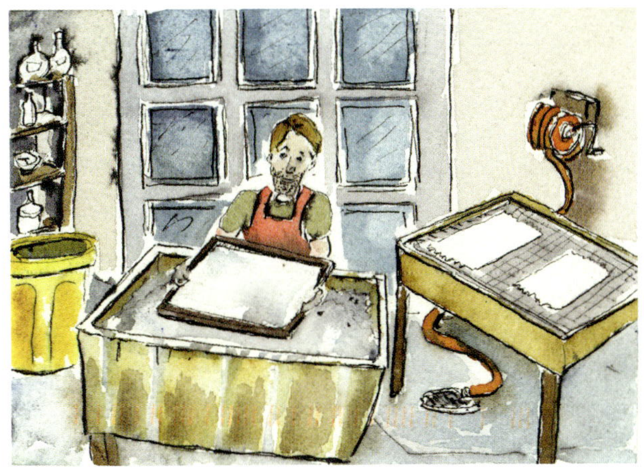

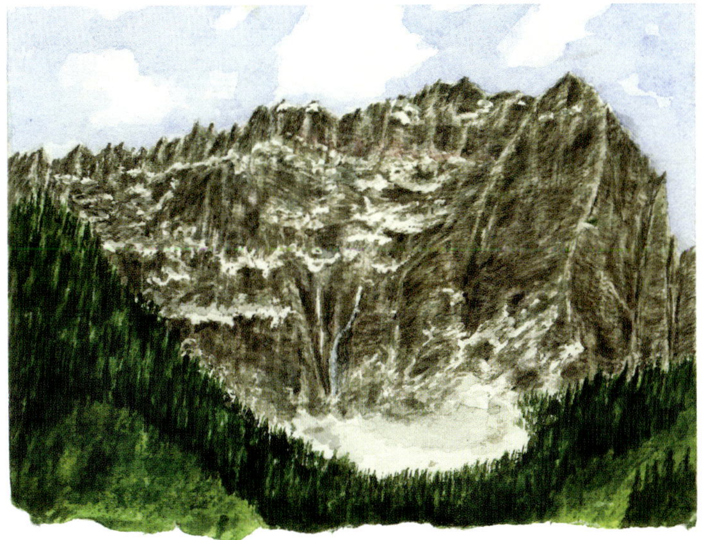

My Summer, 2011, watercolor, 8 1/2 x 6 in. (illustrated; not in exhibition)

bruce
crownover

Master Printer, Tandem Press
UW–Madison Department of Art affiliate, since 1994

1989 Master of Fine Arts, UW–Madison
1986 Bachelor of Fine Arts, Utah State University

Recent career achievements

2011 *Glacial Retreat Project with Todd Anderson*, documentation of glacial retreat in Glacier National Park, Mont.

2011 *Bruce Crownover Paintings & Drawings*, Marina Condos, Madison, Wisc.

2010 *Art Department Adjunct Show*, 7th-floor gallery group exhibition, UW–Madison Art Department

2008 *Bruce Crownover Paintings, Ellen Pollan Monoprints, Steve Agard Photographs*, Gallery 608 at Sundance Cinemas exhibition, Madison, Wisc.

2008 Capitol Lakes solo exhibition, Madison, Wisc.

Works in exhibition

Outlet, 2011, lithograph, 25 x 36 in.

julie
ganser

Director of Advising, Programs and Outreach

UW–Madison Department of Art affiliate, since 2004

2003 Master of Fine Arts, UW–Madison

2002 Master of Arts, UW–Madison

2000 Bachelor of Fine Arts, UW–Madison

Recent career achievements

2011 *Eco-Byway*, Benedicta Arts Center & Saint John's Art Center
group exhibitions, Saint John's University, St. Joseph, Minn.

2011 5th International Marine Debris Conference Digital Exhibition,
Waikiki Marriott, Honolulu, Hawaii

2001 *The Nature of Waste: An Art Meets Science* Digital Exhibition, Petit
Science Center, GSU, Atlanta, Ga.

2010 *Saving the Sanctuary* curator, Freeport Art Museum, Freeport, Ill.

2009 *Deep Winter, Synthetic Summer*, James Watrous Gallery solo exhibition,
Madison, Wisc.

2003 Featured in *New American Paintings*, vol. 47

Works in exhibition

Silo, 2011, recycled plastic, synthetic and natural plant materials,
82 x 136 x 12 in.

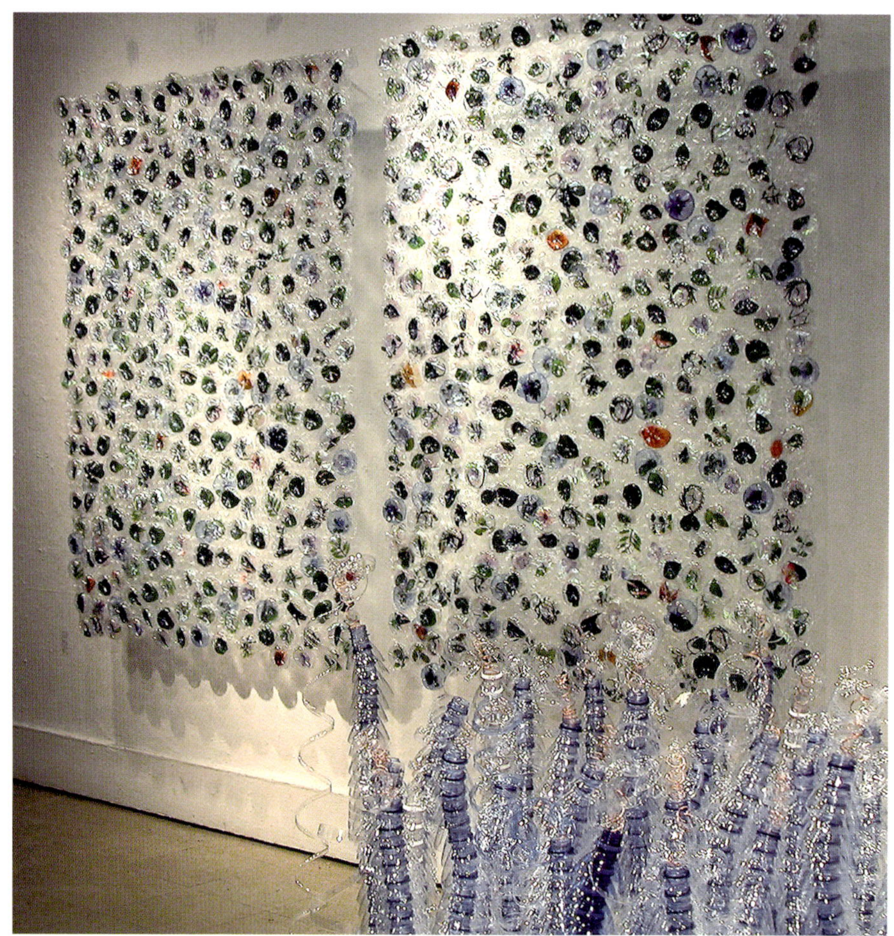

Bubble Garden/No Refill Installation, 2009, mixed recycled materials, 66 x 100 x 8 in.
(illustrated; not in exhibition)

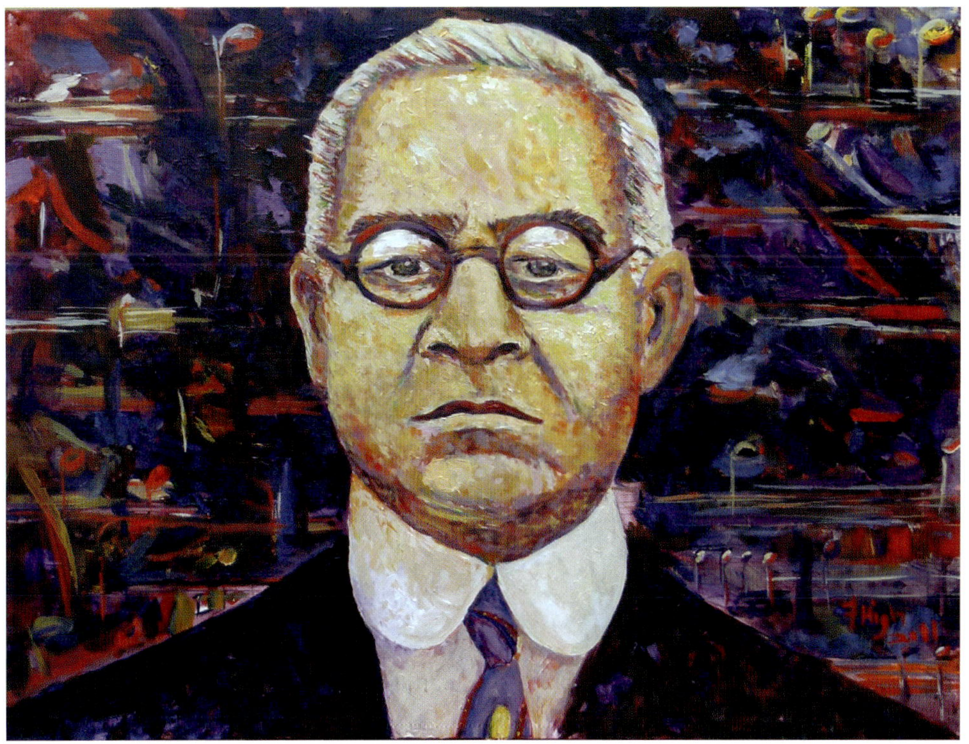

Works in exhibition

Homage to George Washington Comfort (1874–1933): Composer, Band Director of Alcorn A&M College, and My Maternal Great-Grandfather, 2011, acrylic, mixed media, 96 x 80 x 2.5 in.

freida high
w. tesfagiorgis

UW–Madison Afro-American Studies, since 1972

UW–Madison Department of Art affiliate

1971 Master of Fine Arts, UW–Madison

1970 Master of Arts, UW–Madison

1968 Bachelor of Sciences, Northern Illinois University

1966 Associate in Arts, Graceland College

Recent career achievements

2011 Chancellor's Distinguished Teaching Award, UW-Madison

2010 "1897.com: Peju Layiwola's Metamonument." In exhibition catalogue *Benin1897.com: Art and the Restitution Question*, 15-40. (Lagos: WY Foundation)

2010 *African-American Artists Who Teach in Wisconsin Colleges, Universities and Schools* (invitational), Museum of Wisconsin Art exhibition, West Bend, Wisc.

2009 Consultant, Ford Foundation of West Africa, Lagos, Nigeria, Museum Education-National Commission for Museums & Monuments, National Museum

2009 "In Search of a Discourse and Critique/s that Center the Art of Black Women Artists." *The Feminist and Visual Culture Reader*, A. Jones ed. (Routledge)

amy
newell

Academic Curator at Tandem Press

UW–Madison Department of Art affiliate, since 1999

1999 Master of Fine Arts, UW–Madison

1993 Bachelor of Fine Arts, Virginia Commonwealth University

Recent career achievements

2011 Golda Meir Library permanent collection, UW–Milwaukee

2011 United Therapeutic permanent collection, Washington, D.C.

2010 Madison Children's Museum permanent collection, Madison, Wisc.

2007 *Something Clever*, Gardiner Art Gallery solo exhibition, Stillwater, Okla.

2005 *Together With*, Wilson Center for the Arts solo exhibition,
Brookfield, Wisc.

2002 *Souvenirs*, Wisconsin Academy solo exhibition, Madison, Wisc.

Works in exhibition

Cocktail #1, 2011, relief, 2.5 x 2.5 in.

Cocktail #2, 2011, relief, 2.5 x 2.5 in.

Cocktail #3, 2011, relief, 2.5 x 2.5 in.

Cocktail #4, 2011, relief, 2.5 x 2.5 in.

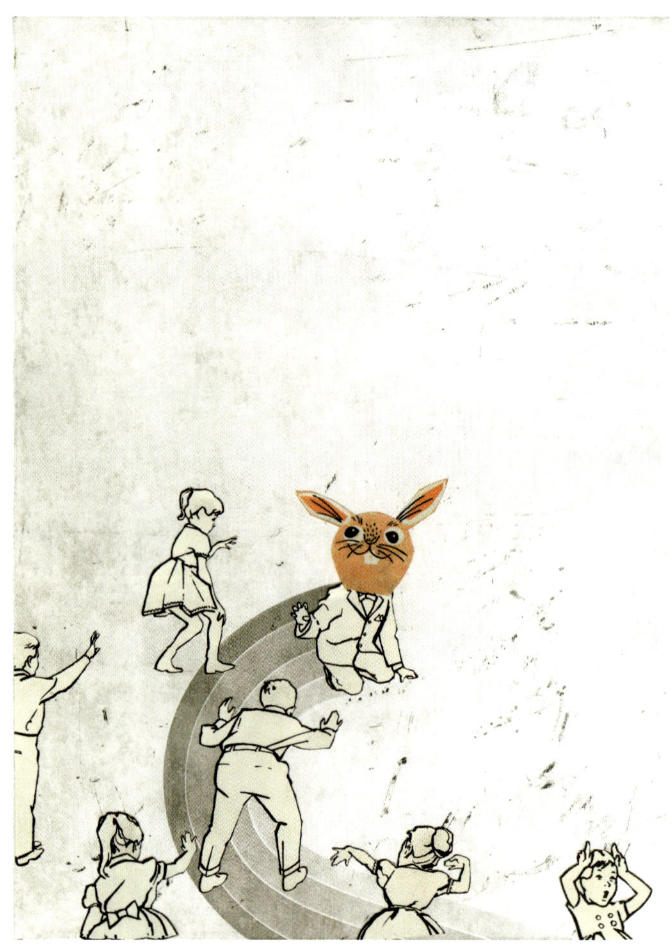

The Scavengers (Amy Newell & Jason Ruhl), *We Walk the Streets at Night*, 2010, etching, relief, digital, collage, 15 x 11 in. (illustrated; not in exhibition)

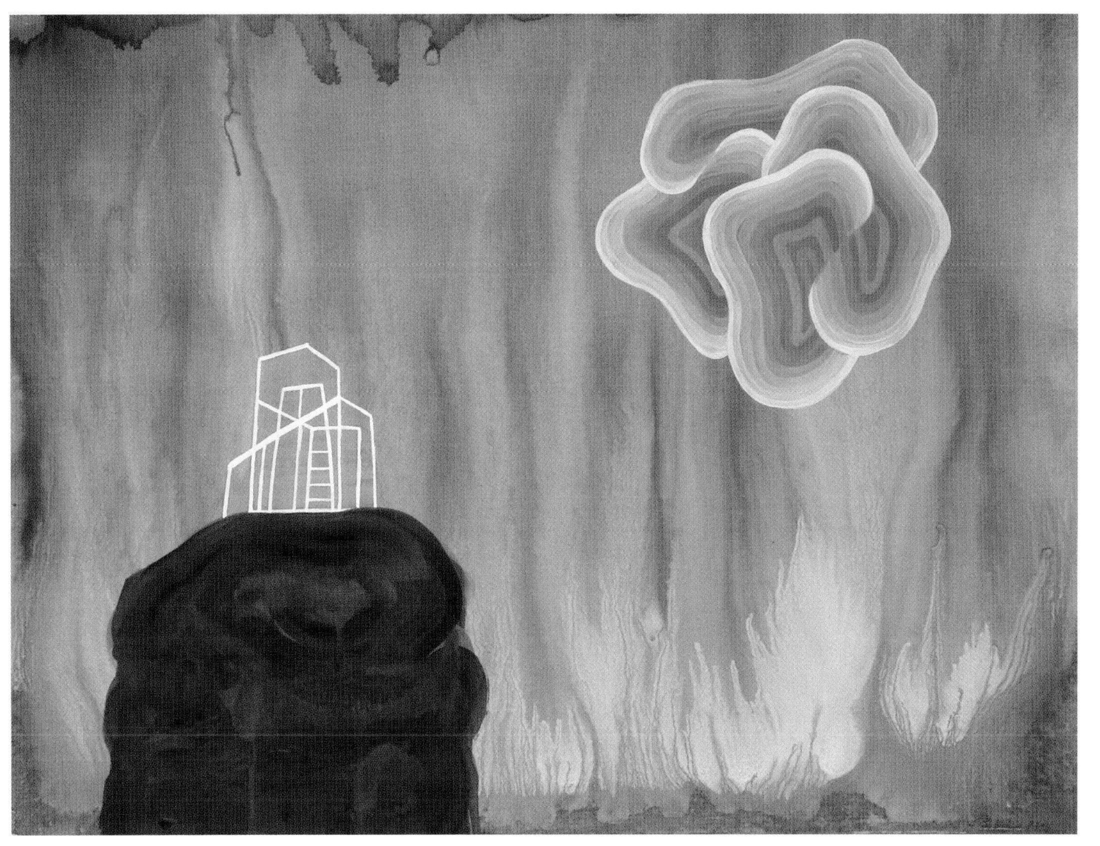

rubin

Master Printer, Tandem Press
UW–Madison Department of Art affiliate, since 1988

1984 Master of Fine Arts, Arizona State University
1978 Bachelor of Fine Arts, Center for Creative Studies, School of
Art and Design, Detroit, Mich.

Recent career achievements

2011 Wisconsin Artists Biennial, Anderson Arts Center,
   Kenosa, Wisc.
2010 Central Academy of Fine Art printmaking workshop,
   Beijing, China
2010 Cashe Show, Madison, Wisc.

Works in exhibition

Styx and Stones, 2011, watercolor and gouache, 18 x 24 in. (illustrated)
Underwater Cloud, 2011, watercolor and gouache, 24 x 18 in.

jason
ruhl

Master Printer, Tandem Press
UW–Madison Department of Art Affiliate, since 2007

2002 Master of Fine Arts, UW–Madison
1999 Bachelor of Fine Arts, Minnesota State University

Recent career achievements

2011 *Epicentro: Re Tracing the Plains,* Dipartimento di Studi Linguistici e
Culturali Comparati group exhibition, University of Ca' Foscari, Venice

2010 *Minnesoter,* CSU Gallery solo exhibition, MSU, Mankato, Minn.

2010 *I Ain't No Goddamn Son of A Bitch,* Domashnaja Galereja group
exhibition, Kiev, Ukraine

2008 *OBJECTIVOS MOVILES/MOVING TARGETS,* Proyecto Ace
group exhibition, Buenos Aires, Argentina

Works in exhibition

Cut & Paste #381, 2011, collage, relief, digital, 12 x 12 in.

Cut & Paste #209, 2011, collage, relief, digital, 9 x 12 in.

Cut & Paste #291, 2011, collage, relief, digital, 16 x 20 in.

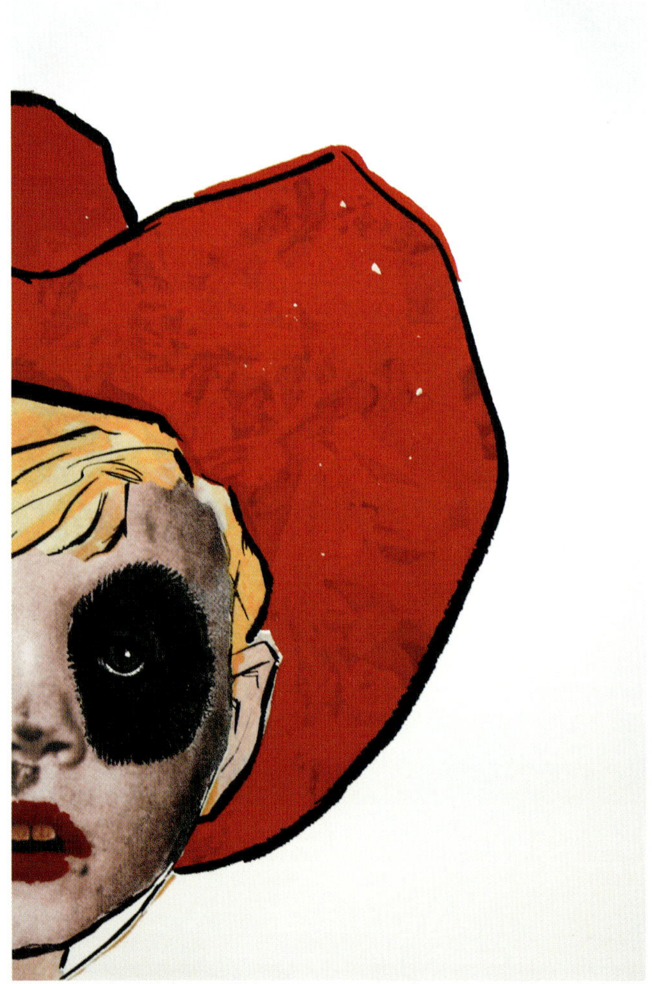

The Scavengers (Amy Newell & Jason Ruhl), *Hit Me with Your
Best Shot,* 2010, lithograph, pochoir, digital, 22 x 30 in.
(illustrated; not in exhibition)

david
becker

Professor Emeritus

UW–Madison Department of Art, 1985–2006

Life Drawing

1965 Master of Fine Arts, University of Illinois, Urbana–Champaign

1961 Bachelor of Science, University of Wisconsin–Milwaukee

Recent career achievements

Represented by Ann Nathan Gallery, Chicago, Ill.

Works in exhibition

No U-Turn, 2010, oil on canvas, 60 x 76 in. (illustrated)

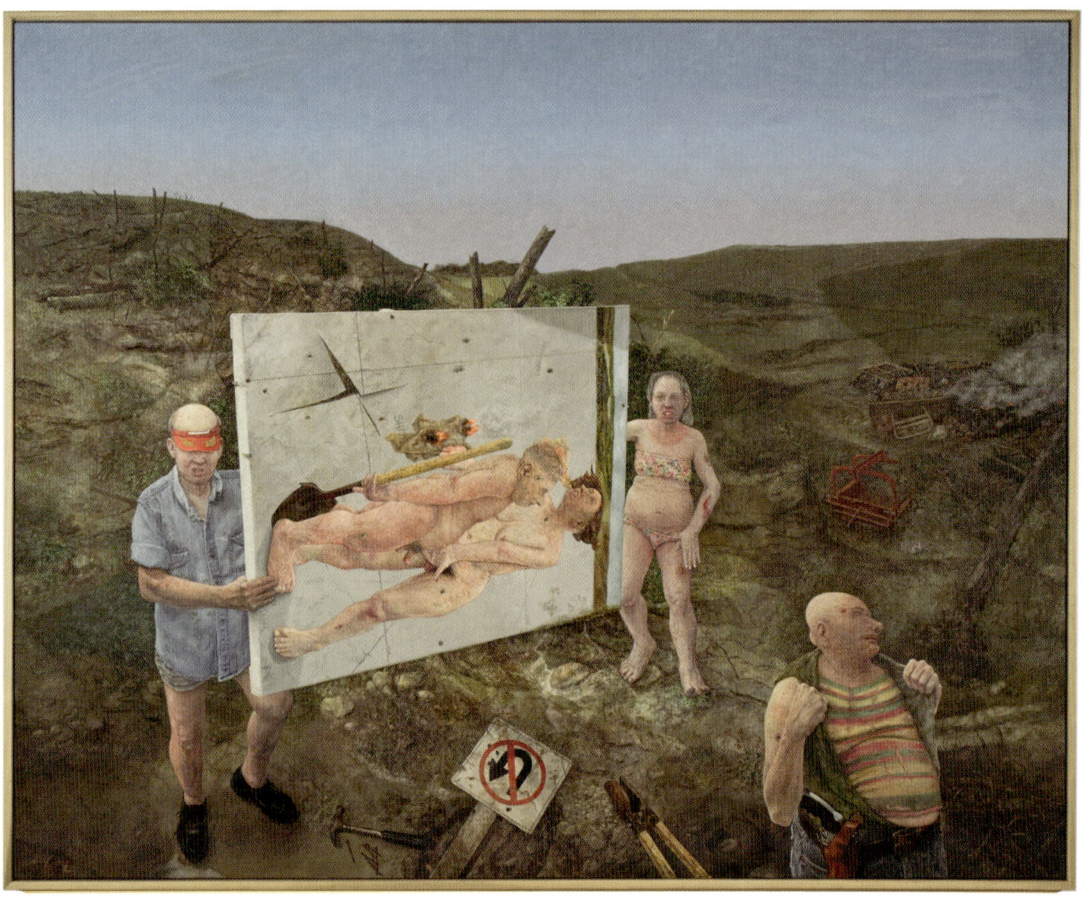

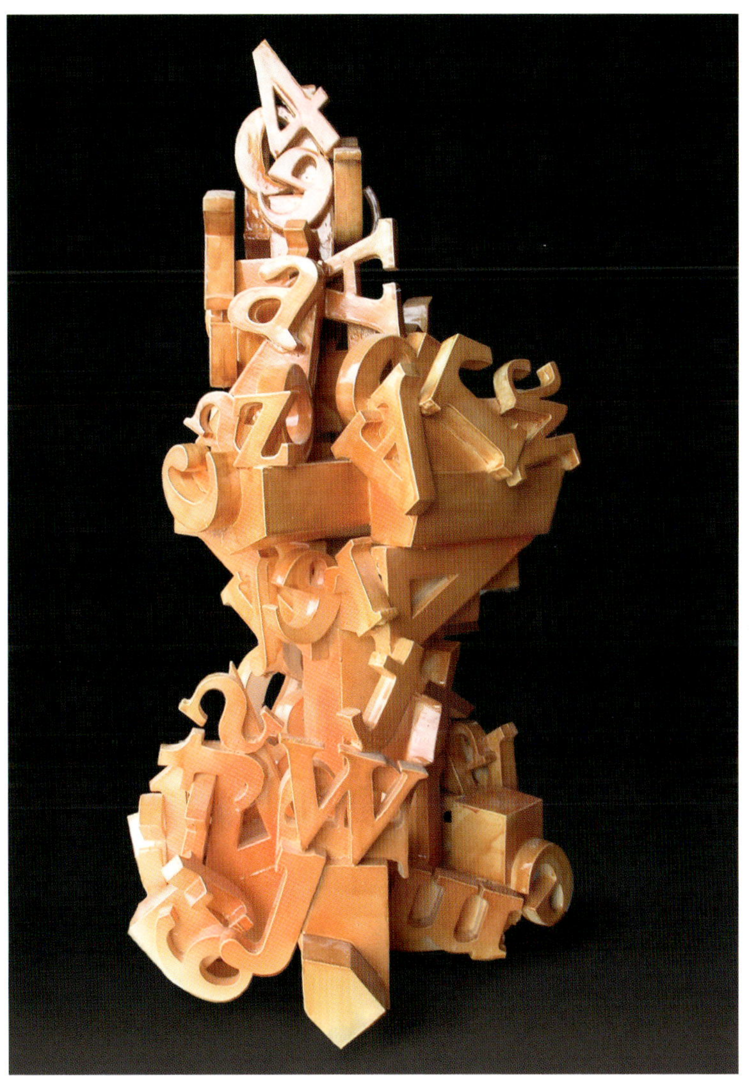

bruce m.
breckenridge

Professor Emeritus
UW–Madison Department of Art, 1968–2006
Ceramics

1960 University of California at Berkeley
1956 Academy of the Grande Chaumiere, Paris, France
1953 Master of Fine Arts, Cranbrook Academy of Art, Bloomfield Hills, Mich.
1952 Bachelor of Science, UW–Milwaukee

Recent career achievements

Reuse/Reinvent/Create, Grace Chosy Gallery, Madison, Wisc.
DeRicci Gallery, Edgewood College, Madison, Wisc.
21st Century Ceramics in the United States and Canada, Canzoni Gallery, Columbus, Ohio
Edinboro National Invitational Exhibition, Edinboro University, Edinboro, Penn.
University of Wisconsin System Ceramics Exhibition, UW–Eau Claire
TILE 95, Concept, Artifact, Ornament, Pewabic Pottery, Detroit, Mich.

Works in exhibitions

Moon Over Miami, 2011, clay, 40 x 20 x 20 in. (illustrated)

mel
butor

Professor Emeritus

UW–Madison Department of Art, 1968–1994

Drawing, Foundations, Painting

1960 Master of Arts, Kent State University

1955 Bachelor of Science in Education, Kent State University

1952 Cleveland Institute of Art

Recent career achievements

Stoughton Mural, Stoughton, Wisc.

Heads, Madison Civic Center solo exhibition, Madison, Wisc.

Pop and Op Print Show, American Federation of Arts Gallery group
exhibition, New York, N.Y.

Optical and Hard Edge, Grippi & Waddell Gallery group exhibition,
New York, N.Y.

Works in exhibition

Dawning, 2004, wood plexiglass, reflective polyester, canvas, pigments,
15 1/2 x 15 1/2 x 4 in. (illustrated)

Electric, 2004, wood plexiglass, reflective polyester, 13 x 13 x 10 1/2 in.

Tunnels, 2005, wood plexiglass, reflective polyester, 15 1/2 x 15 1/2 x 4 in.

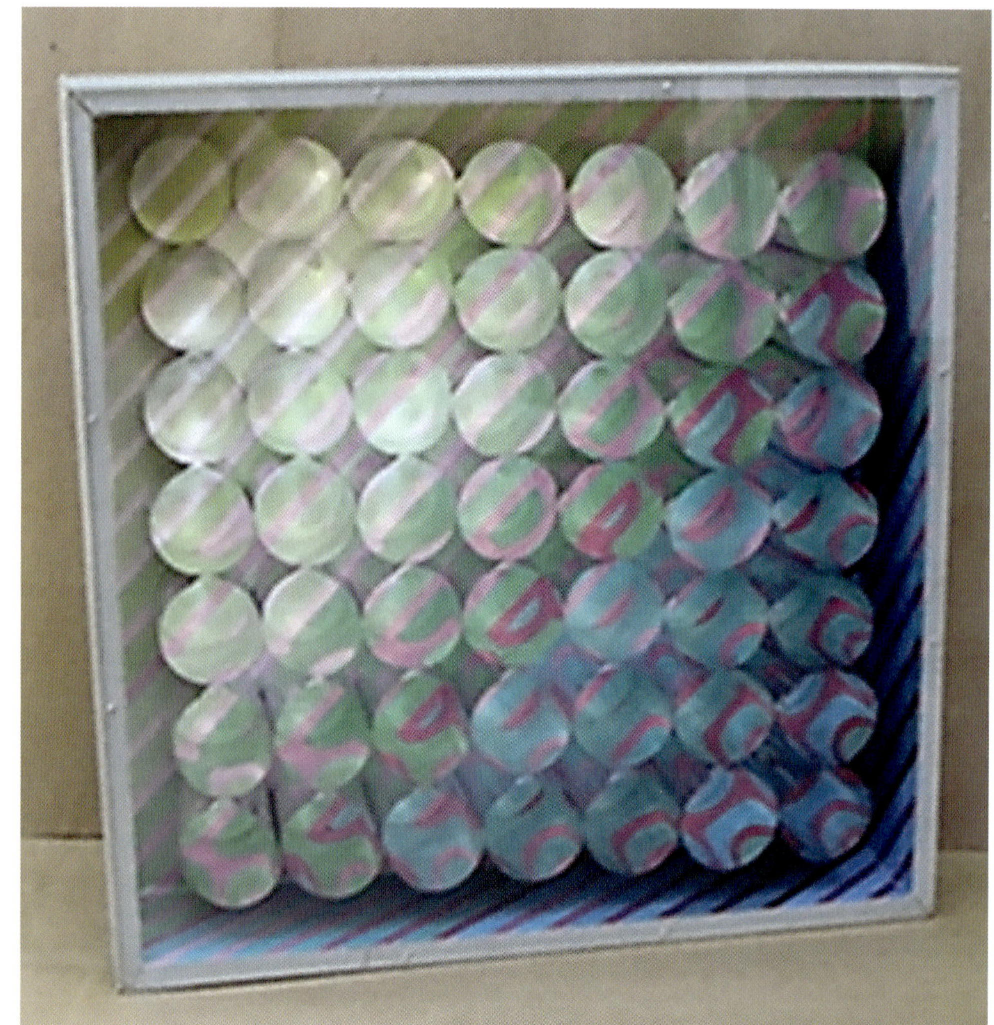

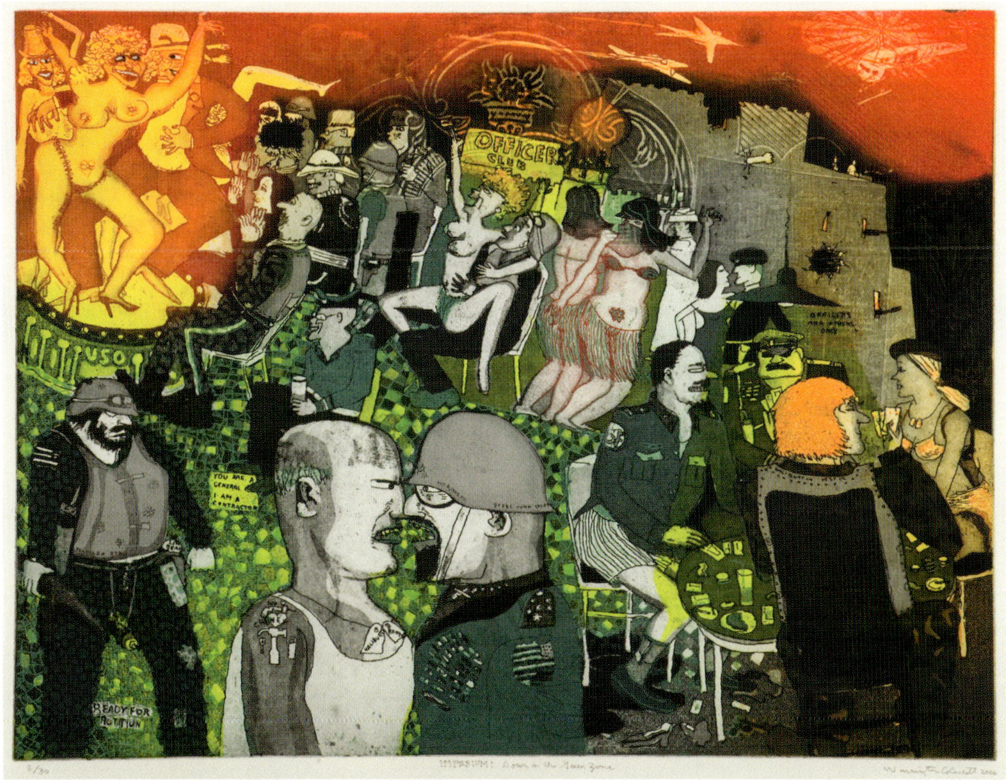

Imperium: Down in the Green Zone, 2009, color etching, 17 x 24 in. (illustrated; not in exhibition)

Works in exhibition

Suite Louisiana: By the Sea, by the Beautiful Sea, 2011, etching, 38 3/8 x 45 in.

warrington
colescott

Professor Emeritus
UW–Madison Department of Art, 1949–1986
Printmaking, Painting

1957 Slade School of Art, University College, University of London
(Fulbright Fellow)
1952 Academie de la Grande Chaumiere, Paris, France
1946 Master of Arts, University of California at Berkeley
1942 Bachelor of Arts, University of California at Berkeley

Recent career achievements

2010 *The Prints of Warrington Colescott—A Catalogue Raisonne 1948–2008*,
Mary Weaver Chapin (Madison: University of Wisconsin Press)
2010 *Out of Line: The Satiric Prints of Warrington Colescott*,
Milwaukee Art Museum solo exhibition, Milwaukee, Wisc.
2010 *The Wisconsin Triennial of Contemporary Art*, Madison Museum of
Contemporary Art group exhibition and catalogue, Madison, Wisc.
2010 *Suite Louisiana: Color Intaglio Prints by Warrington Colescott*, New Orleans
Museum of Art solo exhibition and catalogue, New Orleans, La.
2009 *184th Annual Exhibition of Contemporary American Art*, National
Academy Museum group exhibition and catalogue, New York, N.Y.,
2009 Dessie Grant Greer Prize and Orocelle Lance Award for *Suite
Louisiana: Storyville, The Last Salon*

fred
fenster

Professor Emeritus

UW–Madison Department of Art, 1962–2005

Metalwork

1960 Master of Fine Arts, Cranbrook Academy of Art, Bloomfield
Hills, Mich.

1956 Bachelor of Science, City College of New York, N.Y.

Recent career achievements

2011 One person exhibit, Metal Museum, Memphis Tenn.

2011 Outstanding Artist Educator, Penland School of Crafts Award

2006 Gold medal from American Crafts Council for craftsmanship and
service to the field

2004 James Renwick Alliance award for excellence in teaching art

2002 Hans Christiaansen Memorial Silversmithing award

1995 Elected Fellow of the American Crafts Council

Works in exhibition

Vase, 2011, pewter, 3 1/2 x 14 in. (illustrated)

Kiddush Cup, 2011, sterling and gold plate 3 1/2 x 7 1/4 in.

Bowl, 2011, pewter, 7 1/2 x 7 in.

Salt & Pepper, 2011, pewter

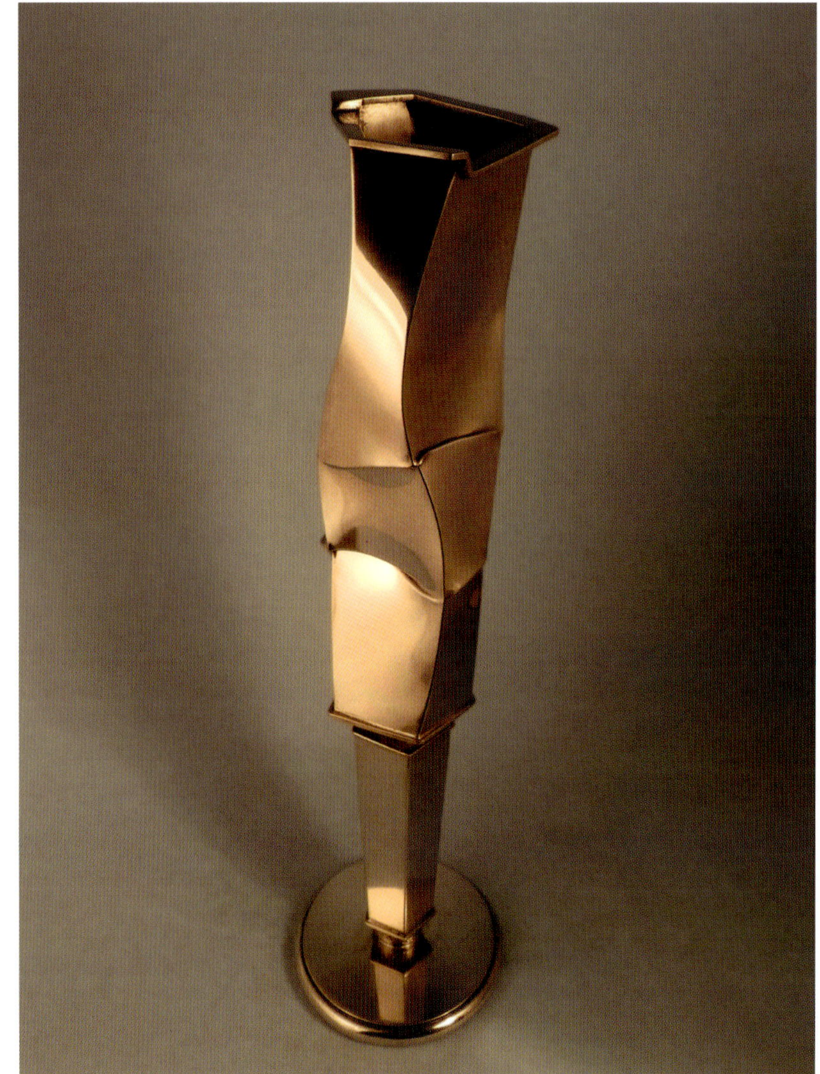

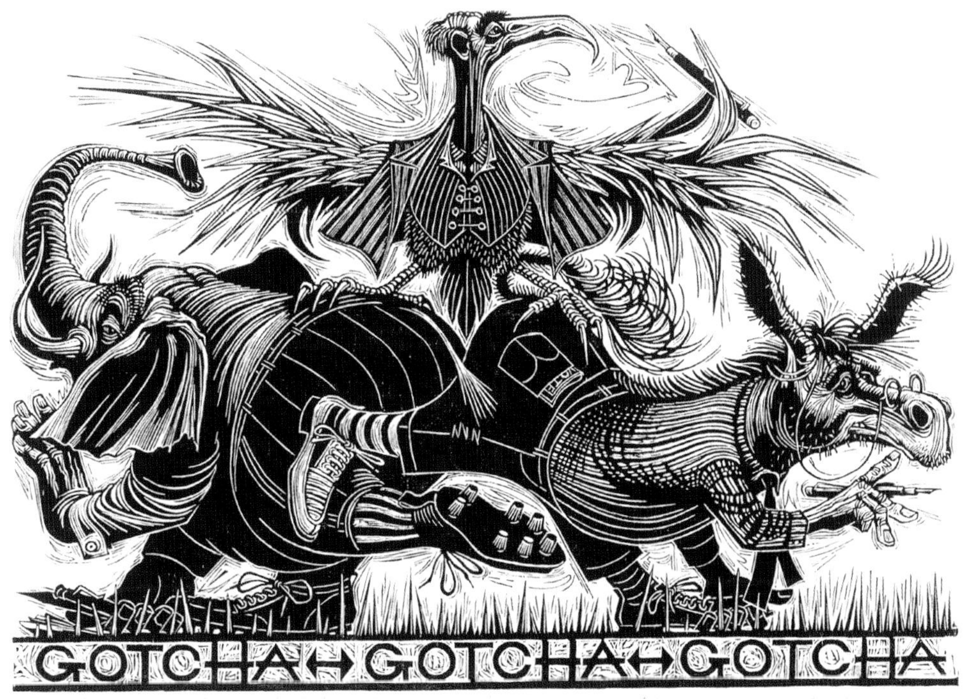

raymond l.
gloeckler

Professor Emeritus

UW–Madison Department of Art, 1961–1997

Woodcut/Wood Engraving, Painting, Art Education

1952 Master of Science, UW–Madison

1950 Bachelor of Science, UW–Madison

Recent career achievements

2010 *Bad Boys, Magic Ladies and Timeless Masters: Contemporary American Woodcuts*, Morgan Art of Papermaking Conservatory and Educational Foundation invitational, Cleveland, Ohio

2010 *The Loaded Image, Printmaking as Persuasion*, Chazen Museum of Art, Madison, Wisc.

2009 The Wisconsin Visual Art Lifetime Achievement Award, presented by the Museum of Wisconsin Art, the Wisconsin Academy of Sciences, Arts and Letters, and the Wisconsin Visual Artists

2008 *The American Biennial Exhibition of Contemporary Miniature Prints International*, University of Iowa and University of Texas

2004 *Woodcuts by Ray Gloeckler*, Chazen Museum of Art solo retrospective and catalogue, Madison, Wisc.

2002 Fellow of the Wisconsin Academy of Sciences, Arts and Letters

2001 *Raymond Gloeckler: Engravers Cut*, Primrose Academy Ltd., (Bicester: England)

Works in exhibition

No Matter Who You Vote For, The Government Wins, woodcut, 16 1/2 x 24 in. (illustrated)

phillip
hamilton

Professor Emeritus

UW–Madison Department of Art, 1964–2004

Graphic Design

1964 Master of Fine Arts, Indiana University

1961 Bachelor of Science, University of Cincinnati

Recent career achievements

2010 *Four Decades of Book, Logo, Poster & Publication Design*, Portage
Center for the Arts retrospective exhibition, Portage, Wisc.

2010 Ten-Year Dane County Cultural Affairs Commission Art Calendar
Retrospective, Overture Center and Dane County Regional Airport,
Madison, Wisc.

2006 Installation of "W" floor inset, Dane County Regional Airport
Terminal, Madison, Wisc.

2002 Printing Industries of America award for Dane County Cultural
Affairs Commission calendar

2001 School of Education Faculty Distinguished Achievement Award

1999 Gerald Bartell Award for the Arts

Works in exhibition

Poster for retrospective exhibition *Four Decades of Book, Logo, Poster &
Publication Design*, 2010, 36 x 24 in. (illustrated)

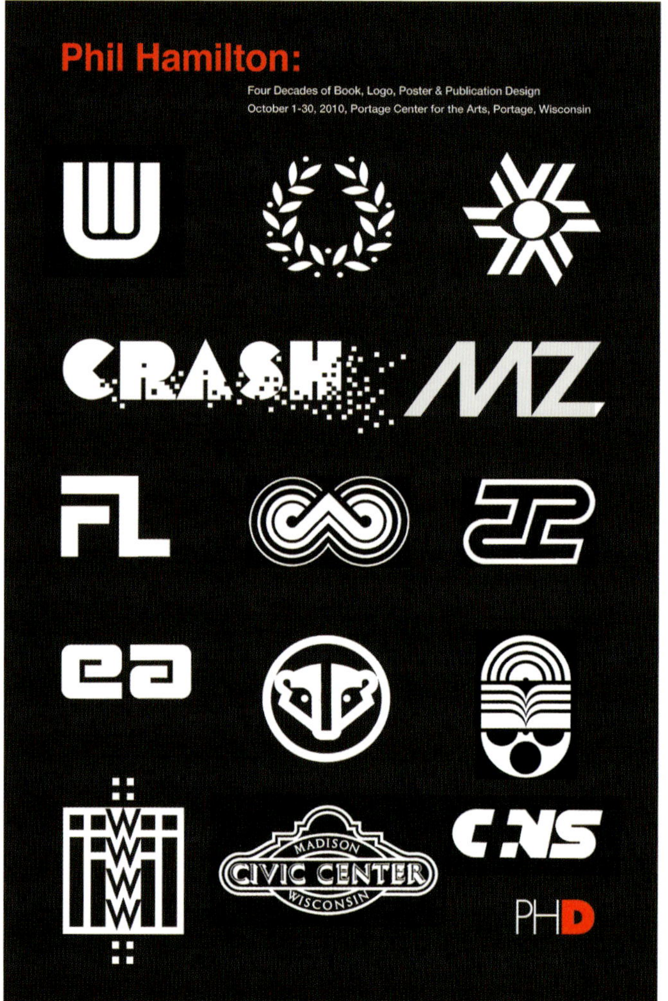

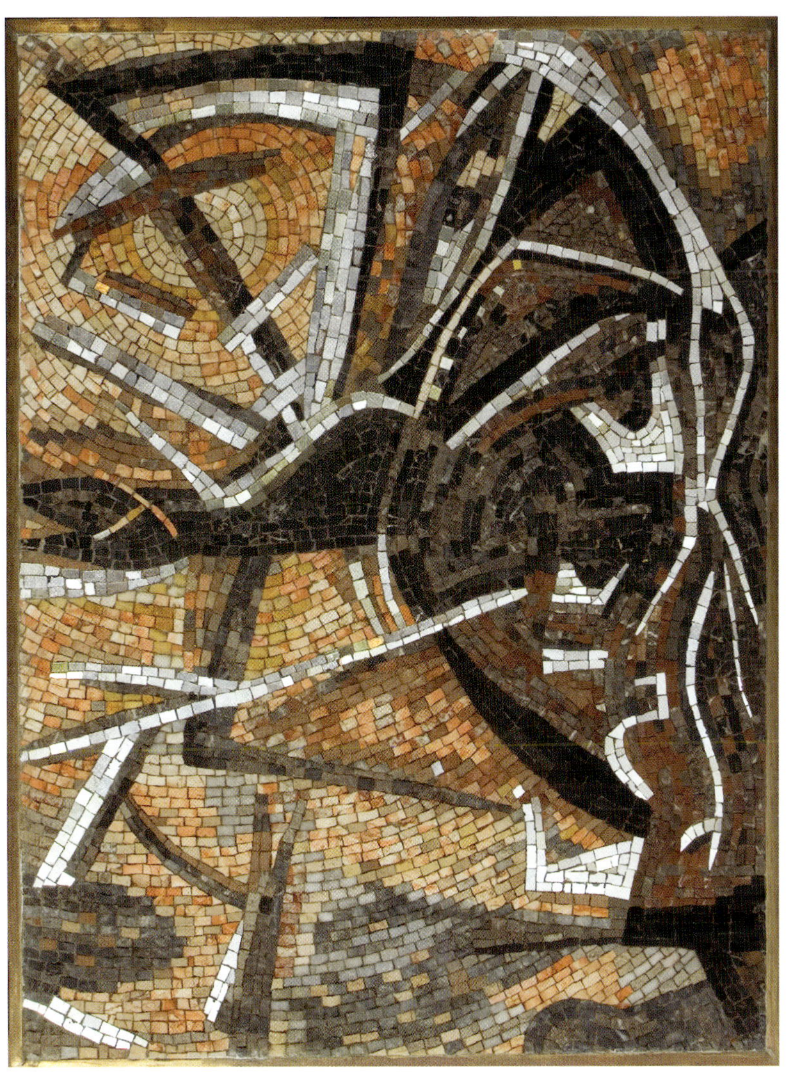

marjorie
kreilick

Professor Emerita

UW–Madison Department of Art, 1953–1991

Sculpture

1963 FAAR, American Academy in Rome, Rome, Italy

1952 Master of Fine Arts, Cranbrook Academy of Art

1947 Master of Arts, Ohio State University

1946 Bachelor of Arts, Ohio State University

Recent career achievements

2009 *Sunrise* acquired by the Flint Institute of Art, Flint, Mich.

1969 *Blossoms Changed the World* architectural commission, Mayo Clinic, Rochester, Minn.

1967 *Disc for Foucault* architectural commission, Augustana College, Sioux Falls, S.D.

1963 *Wisc. Typography* architectural commission, Milwaukee State Office Building, Milwaukee, Wisc.

Works in exhibition

Flight Forward, 2008, smalti and marble tessera, 25 x 18 3/4 x 3/8 in. (illustrated)

richard
lazzaro

Professor Emeritus

UW–Madison Department of Art, 1963–98

2-D, Painting

1963 Master of Fine Arts, University of Illinois at Urbana–Champaign

1961 Bachelor of Fine Arts, Kent State University

1959 Diploma, Cleveland Institute of Art

Recent career achievements

2011 *Richard Lazzaro: Visual Verses*, Butler Institute of American Art, Youngstown, Ohio

2011 *Richard Lazzaro: Gouache Paintings*, Calvin Charles Gallery, Scottsdale, Ariz.

2010 *Intuitive Abstraction: Visual, Lyrical Poetry*, Calvin Charles Gallery, Scottsdale, Ariz.

2006 *Intuitive Abstraction*, Overture Center for the Arts, Madison, Wisc.

2005 *Fourth International Tsai-mo Invitational Exhibition*, Da-Dun Gallery, TaiChung Cultural Affairs Bureau, Taichung, Taiwan

2003–2006 *Pivot Points: Six Painters, Six Poets*, traveling exhibition

Works in exhibition

Marianna's Voyage, 2011, gouache, 36 x 30 in. (illustrated)

Random Passages, 2011, gouache, 29 x 41 in.

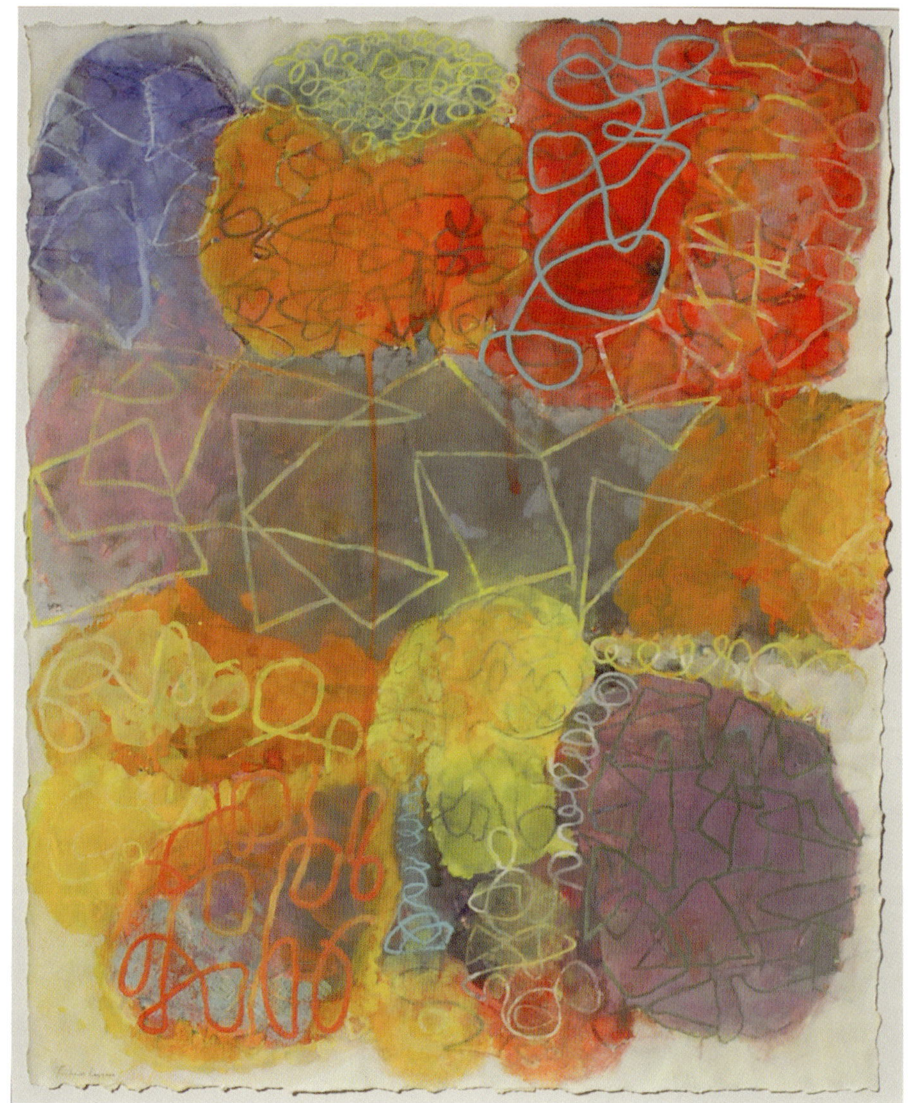

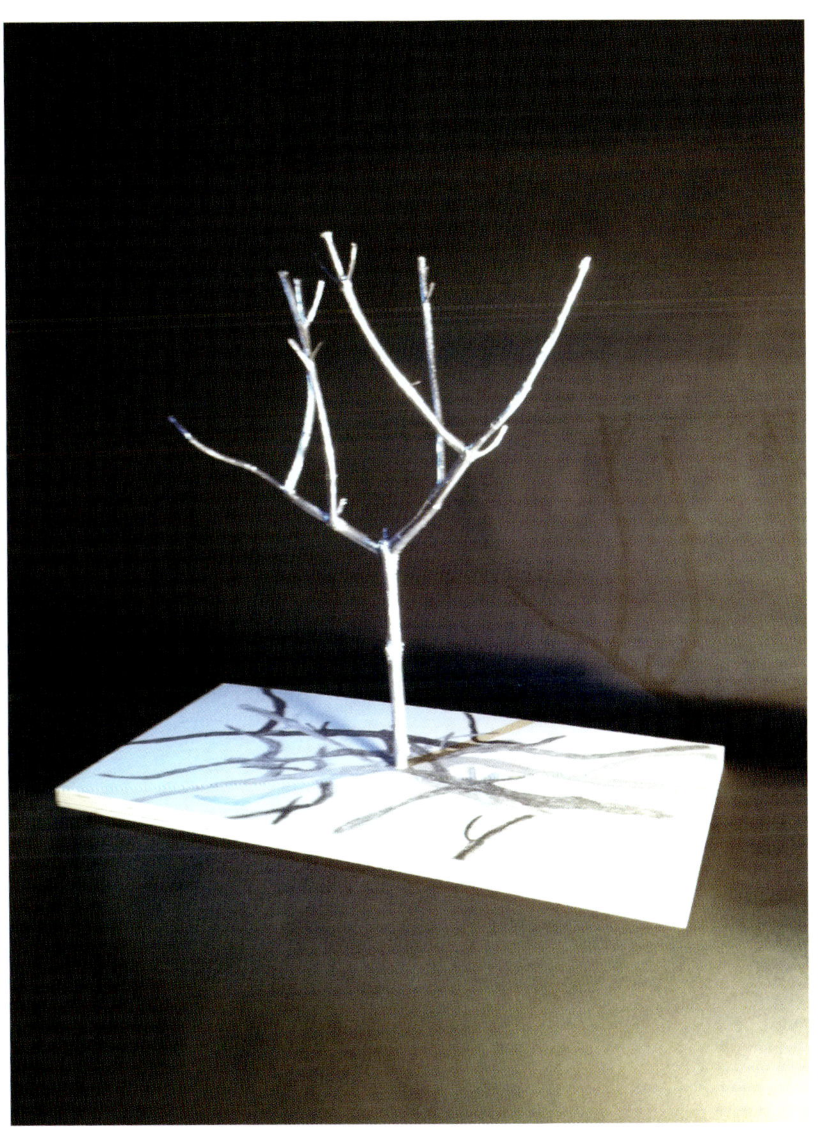

truman
lowe

Professor Emeritus
UW–Madison Department of Art, 1975–2010
Sculpture

1973 Master of Fine Arts UW–Madison
1969 Bachelor of Science UW–La Crosse

Recent career achievements

2008 Fritz Scholder: *Indian/Not Indian*, Exhibition at the Smithsonian Institution National Museum of the American Indian (NMAI), Washington, D.C. and Manhattan, N.Y.

2007 Wisconsin Visual Art Lifetime Achievement Award

2005 Sciences, Arts, and Letters Academy Fellow of Wisconsin selected member

2004 Jo Ortel, *Woodland Reflections, the Art of Truman Lowe* (Madison, Wisc: University of Wisconsin Press)

2004 *Native Modernism: The Art of George Morrison and Allan Houser*, catalogue editor and exhibition curator, National Museum of the American Indian, Smithsonian Institution, Washington, D.C.

2000 Curator of contemporary art, National Museum of the American Indian, Smithsonian Institution, Washington, D.C.

Works in exhibition

Shadow series no. 8, 2011, paper, wood, charcoal and paint, 18 1/2 x 11 1/4 x 22 in. (illustrated)

eleanor
moty

Professor Emerita

UW–Madison Department of Art, 1972–2001

Art Metals, Jewelry, Metalsmithing

1971 Master of Fine Arts, Tyler School of Art, Temple University

1968 Bachelor of Fine Arts, University of Illinois at Urbana–Champaign

Recent career achievements

2012 *Master Metalsmith*, Metal Museum solo exhibition, Memphis, Tenn.

2011 *21st Century Jewelry, The Best of the 500 Series*, Marthe Le Van
(New York: Lark Crafts)

2010 *20/20* alumni metals invitational exhibition, School of Art + Design,
University of Illinois at Champaign–Urbana, Champaign, Ill.

2010 *Jewelry by Artists: In the Studio 1940–2000*, Kelly H. L'Ecuyer (Boston:
MFA Publications)

2009 *Metals/Jewelry/CAD-CAM Master of Fine Arts Alumni Exhibition,
1969–2009*, Stella Elkins Tyler Gallery, Tyler School of Art, Temple
University, Philadelphia, Penn.

2008 *New Work, Eleanor Moty*, Perimeter Gallery solo exhibition,
Chicago, Ill.

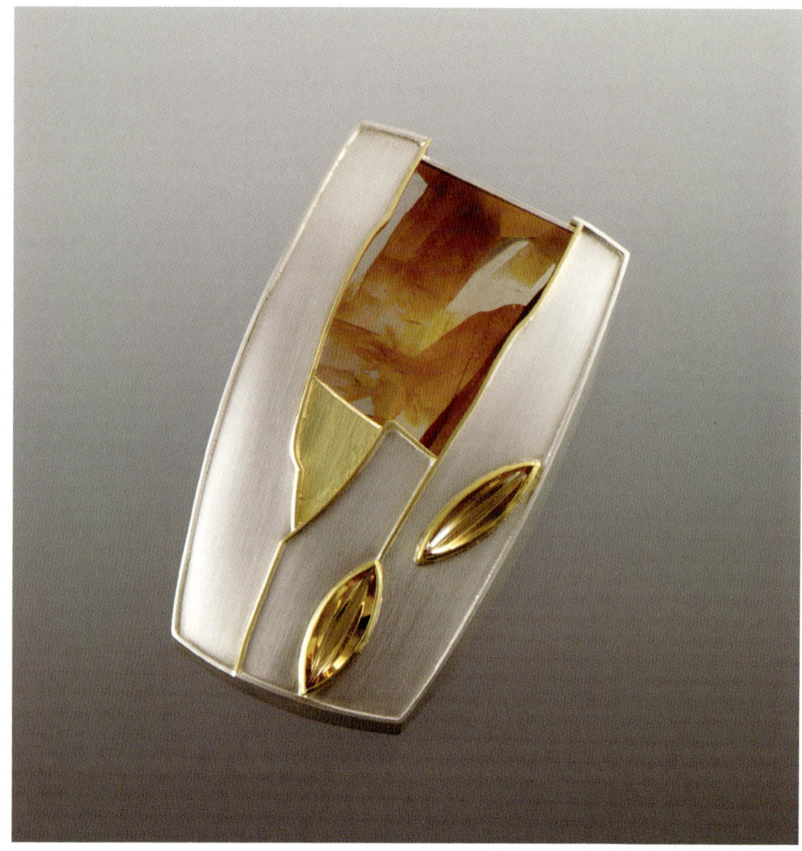

Works in exhibition

"Autumn Veil" Brooch, 2008, sterling silver, 22K and 18K gold, quartz with
iron inclusions, citrines, 2 7/8 x 1 5/8 x 1/2 in. (illustrated)

"Crystal Void" Brooch, 2009, sterling silver, 18K, 14K gold, phantom
quartz, 2 1/8 x 2 1/4 x 3/8 in.

"Aerial View" Brooch, 2011, sterling silver, 14K gold, phantom quartz,
2 1/8 x 2 3/8 x 5/8 in.

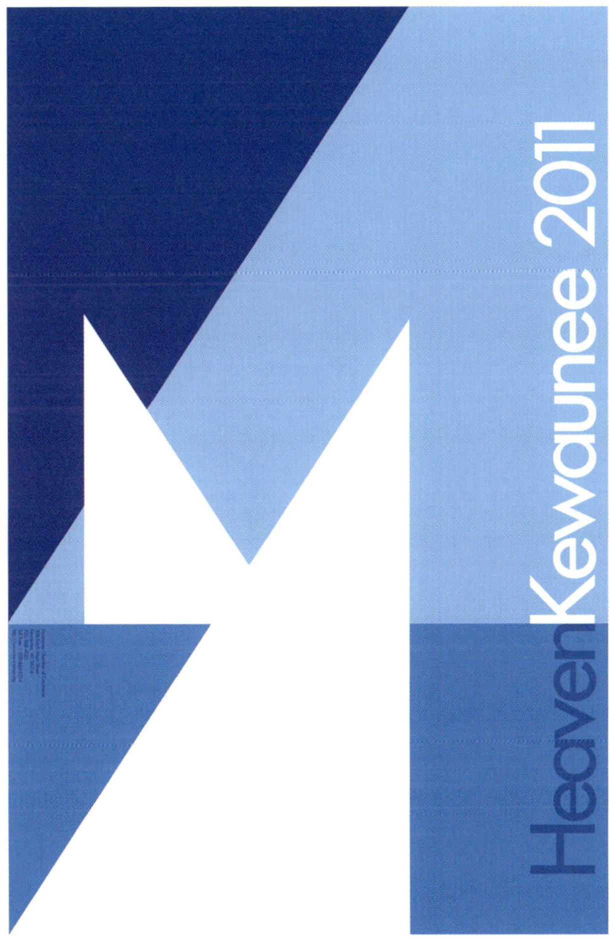

Kewaunee Heaven 2011, 2010, digital ink jet, 24 x 30 in.
(illustrated; not in exhibition)

john r.
rieben

Professor Emeritus
UW–Madison Department of Art, 1989–2006
Graphic Design

1966 Master of Fine Arts, Indiana University
1961 Master of Science, Indiana University
1957 Bachelor of Science, University of Michigan–Ann Arbor

Recent career achievements

2011 *Symbol*, Steven Bateman and Angus Hyland (Laurence King
   Publishers)
2011, 2010, 2009 *Graphis* poster annuals
2009 *UNIMARK International, The Design of Business and the Business of
   Design*, Jan Conradi (Baden, Switzerland: Lars Müller Publishers)
2011, 2010, 2009, 2008 Dunedin Fine Art Center annual art exhibition
   Dunedi, Fla.
2009 *2 Views*, Studio 1403 Gallery 2-person exhibition, Clearwater, Fla.
2007–2008 *50 Years of Helvetica*, Museum of Modern Art group exhibition,
   New York, N.Y.

Works in exhibition

The 39 Steps, 2011, digital ink jet, 30 x 40 in.